Twayne's United States Authors Series

Sylvia E. Bowman, *Editor*

INDIANA UNIVERSITY

Maxwell Anderson

TUSAS 279

Maxwell Anderson

MAXWELL ANDERSON

By ALFRED S. SHIVERS

Stephen F. Austin State University

TWAYNE PUBLISHERS

A DIVISION OF G. K. HALL & CO., BOSTON

Library of Congress Cataloging in Publication Data

Shivers, Alfred S
    Maxwell Anderson.

(Twayne's United States authors series; TUSAS 279)
Bibliography: p. 163–70
Includes index.
1. Anderson, Maxwell, 1888–1959.
PS3501.N256Z9   812'.5'2   [B]   76–24867
ISBN 0-8057-7179-4

For my book-loving sons,

John Samuel
Ralph Allen
Paul Alfred.

May they learn to love the theater, too.

Contents

About the Author

Publications by Dr. Alfred Samuel Shivers have appeared in *Saturday Review, The American Book Collector, Alaska Review, The Dalhousie Review, Bulletin of Bibliography, Milwaukee Journal, Rocky Mountain News,* and elsewhere. They include articles on Jack London, Nathaniel Hawthorne, Federico Lorca; seven short stories; and miscellaneous book reviews. His most important scholarly publication until now has been the critical-analytical book *Jessamyn West,* published in 1972 by Twayne Publishers. Aside from being a literary critic, Dr. Shivers is also an amateur horticulturist: he has published articles on rabbiteye blueberries and muscadine grapes in *Organic Gardening and Farming* magazine.

Dr. Shivers has taught courses in American and English literature at Wisconsin State College (Superior), Colorado State University, Northern Illinois University, and Stephen F. Austin State University. He is now full professor, and he specializes in late-nineteenth-and-twentieth-century American literature, especially drama.

Following service in both the U.S. Army and Air Force, he earned the B. A. and M. A. degrees in English (University of Florida), and the Ph. D. in English (Florida State University).

He first became interested in Maxwell Anderson while teaching Anderson's *Four Verse Plays* to undergraduates in Illinois. The present book was made possible by a Faculty Research Grant awarded by Stephen F. Austin State University.

Preface

Published scholarship has scarcely recognized the major contribution to American drama of Maxwell Anderson's pioneering efforts that were overshadowed only perhaps by Eugene O'Neill. This most extensive of the book-length studies published thus far on Anderson assimilates not only the relevant published research, but also the significant oral and unpublished written sources that illuminate the life and especially the art of this great man. The book offers to readers a careful, accurate, and analytical account.

Anderson was a shy man and most reluctant early in his career to grant interviews to people writing about him, as Barrett H. Clark regretfully notes in *An Hour of American Drama* (1930); for Anderson claimed that the author who once began to talk about himself was in effect already dead and food for worms. But, as I indicate in this book, he finally relented and granted a few — but only a few — interviews. He left no autobiography as such except for one open letter of reminiscence that he penned four months before his death, and that was subsequently printed in the *University of North Dakota Alumni Review* of December 5, 1958. Otherwise, he released to the public only fragmentary and scattered glimpses of his personal life. So formidable have been the difficulties in learning about his life that the only four books devoted exclusively to him — Barrett H. Clark's *Maxwell Anderson, The Man and His Plays* (1933), Mabel D. Bailey's published doctoral dissertation *Maxwell Anderson The Playwright as Prophet* (1957), Martha Cox's *Maxwell Anderson Bibliography* (1958), and Laurence G. Avery's *A Catalogue of the Maxwell Anderson Collection at the University of Texas* (1968) — include next to nothing in the way of biography. The same observation applies to John F. Wharton's remarks about Anderson in *Life among the Playwrights* (1974), which tells a little about the personalities in The Playwrights' Producing Company to which Anderson belonged. This present book intends to make amends for this gap in our knowledge about the *vita* of the dramatist, but it is primarily concerned with his literary contributions.

Chapter 1, which follows Anderson's career in chronological order, explains his theory and artistic practices insofar as these can be
known. Chapter 2 examines Anderson's several war plays of the late
1930's and 1940's that caused the news media to refer to him as a war
dramatist. Chapter 3 discusses those historical plays that deal not
with war primarily but with the corruption of power among emperors, monarchs, and public officials from antiquity to modern
times. Chapter 4 takes up a miscellany of nonhistorical works that
have American settings in the nineteenth and twentieth centuries,
and whose characters are civilians beyond the pale of battlefield,
palace, and elected assembly. Lastly, Chapter 5 discusses various
characteristics of Anderson's plays in an attempt to reach conclu-
sions about his achievement and about his significant contribution to
the dramatic literature of the world.

Within these limitations, I have included for study twenty-three
Anderson plays — more than half the published ones — in order
not only to discuss those that are by general consent outstanding but
to present a sufficiently representative sample of Anderson's dramatic art. The limitations have also given me no alternative but to omit
or give only passing notice to practically all of the complete yet
artistically unsuccessful or uninteresting plays and to all the radio
and television scripts: *The Buccaneer*, "Christmas Carol," "The Day
the Money Stopped," *First Flight*, *The Feast of Ortolans*, "Gypsy,"
Journey to Jerusalem, *Letter to Jackie*, *Lost in the Stars*, *The Miracle
of the Danube*, *Night over Taos*, *Outside Looking In*, *Saturday's
Children*, *Second Overture*, "The White Desert," and *Your Navy*.
The foregoing works are surely minor when they are measured by
any sound standard of judgment. Because I could not locate a copy
of "A Holy Terror," or even a plot summary of it, I was unable to do
more than merely list this obscure piece. Of the complete but professionally unproduced plays I chose to cover only "Sea-Wife,"
which has distinct artistic merit, and to give only brief mention to
"The Masque of Queens" and "Richard and Anne" in those places
where they compare with or illustrate other matters under discussion. These last two items have only minor interest in themselves.
In general, however, the reader's limited access to the unpublished
works made me for that reason alone, if nothing else, hesitate to
discuss them. Except for *What Price Glory*, "Sea-Wife," and *Gods
of the Lightning*, I excluded items from Anderson's apprentice
period of the 1920's and concentrated upon later ones of the period

1930–1959, wherein the mature work, including the masterpieces, may be found.

The situation is somewhat different with Anderson's dramatic criticism because there is much in this important body of material that relates to his own theory and practice in the craft of playwriting. Once again, considerations of space prevented me from treating the poems except incidentally, even though a few of them are interesting in themselves.

ALFRED S. SHIVERS

Stephen F. Austin State University
Nacogdoches, Texas

Acknowledgments

The two persons to whom I owe the largest debt for the biographical information that was hardest to obtain are Lela A. Chambers and Alan Haskett Anderson, the sister and the son of the playwright, who through their letters and other communications helped me immeasurably. Both read an earlier version of the first chapter and offered a generous quantity of corrections and additions which I was able to utilize within the editorial limitations of the book. As the unofficial "family historian," Mrs. Chambers proved to be an alert, detailed, and articulate source of information about Anderson's early years. Alan Anderson, who is a former stage manager and theatrical director, gave me much valuable insight into the professional years, including miscellaneous material about Anderson's addresses, hobbies, recreations, dress, tastes, and writing habits. I have been extremely fortunate in obtaining the cooperation of these two generous people whose respective accounts neatly complemented each other. The requirements of the book, however, allowed me to make use of only a portion of their contributions. Dr. Quentin Anderson, the artist's eldest son, also helped me.

Among the non-relatives who knew Anderson personally, the following helped me with letters of information: Lynn Fontanne (Genessee Depot, Wisconsin); Dr. Lee Norvelle (Indiana University); Dr. C. L. Robertson (Jamestown, North Dakota); Victor Samrock (New York City), formerly the business manager of The Playrights' Producing Company; and John F. Wharton (New York City), formerly legal counsel for and member of the foregoing company. Among the various scholars to whom I am indebted for letters and other assistance are: Dr. Laurence G. Avery (University of North Carolina); Dr. Charles W. Cooper (Santa Barbara, Calif.); Dr. John P. Hagan (Alley Theatre, Houston, Texas); and Dr. Louis G. Geiger (Colorado College). Dr. Paul S. Smith (formerly president of Whittier College) provided useful information germane to that furnished by Cooper. Dr. Edwin W. Gaston, Jr. (my colleague at Stephen F. Austin State University) did me the kindness of reading the manuscript and offering helpful suggestions for improvement.

Then there are scholars not cited in the Notes and References or Selected Bibliography sections whose published writings on tragedy have assisted me: David Daiches, R. J. Dorius, Northrop Frye, Dorothea Krook, Allardyce Nicoll, and Richard B. Sewell. For other kindnesses and services too various to be detailed here, I wish to thank Robert M. Adams, Mary R. O'Loughlin, Gretchen Marz, Clare Sammis (my ever-considerate and beloved mother-in-law), and Robert C. Seymour.

Also I am obligated to several librarians for their patient assistance in supplying copies of documents and other materials: Miss Cleo B. Kelley, Mrs. Julia (Jewdi) Mach, Mrs. Ann H. Prassel, Mr. C. W. Romans, and Miss Jan C. Todd (Stephen F. Austin State University); Mr. J. W. Bird (University of North Dakota); Mrs. Mary M. Hirth (University of Texas); Mrs. Susan R. Rosenberg (Stanford University); and the staff of The State Historical Society of Wisconsin (Madison, Wisconsin).

Although Chapter three is devoted to the topic of corruption by power, this book bears absolutely no indebtedness to Susan Jere White's masters thesis "Corruption of Power in the Plays of Maxwell Anderson," which she submitted to Stephen F. Austin State University in 1974 before my book was first published. The two works are quite independent of each other. Miss White, a student of mine, received her topic from me after my entire manuscript was substantively complete; and of this manuscript she read only Chapter one.

Had it not been for a Faculty Research Grant awarded to me by Stephen F. Austin State University for the summer of 1970, this book would have been much delayed. For this aid I am especially grateful.

I can never sufficiently thank my wife, Clare Ann, who with the children endured as well as she could my long absences from the family circle. She wanted this work done as much as I did.

Chronology

1921   Moves to New City; lives summers in old farmhouse on thirty acres of wilderness land.
1923   "White Desert."
1924   *What Price Glory* with Laurence Stallings. Resigns from *World*.
1925   *Outside Looking In. First Flight* and *The Buccaneer* with Laurence Stallings. *You Who Have Dreams* (poems).
1927   *Saturday's Children.* "Gypsy."
1928   *Gods of the Lightning* with Harold Hickerson. Buys house on 112th street in New York City.
1930   *Elizabeth the Queen.*
1931   Margaret Haskett Anderson dies of stroke in February.
1932   *Night over Taos.*
1933   *Both Your Houses* — wins Pulitzer Prize. Marries Gertrude (Mab) Maynard. *Mary of Scotland.*
1934   *Valley Forge.*
1935   *Winterset* — wins Drama Critics Circle Award.
1936   *The Wingless Victory.*
1937   Wins Drama Critics Circle Award for *High Tor. The Masque of Kings. The Star-Wagon. The Feast of Ortolans.*
1938   *Second Overture. Knickerbocker Holiday* with Kurt Weill.
1939   *Key Largo. The Essence of Tragedy and Other Footnotes and Papers.*
1940   *Journey to Jerusalem.*
1941   *Candle in the Wind. The Miracle of the Danube.*
1942   Travels to Ft. Bragg, North Carolina, to collect background material for *The Eve of St. Mark* (staged later that year). *Your Navy. The Bases of Artistic Creation* (literary criticism).
1943   Travels to North Africa to collect background material for *Storm Operation. Letter to Jackie.*
1944   *Storm Operation.*
1946   *Joan of Lorraine. Truckline Cafe.*
1947   *Off Broadway Essays about the Theatre.* Travels to Greece.
1948   *Anne of the Thousand Days.*
1949   *Lost in the Stars* with Kurt Weill.
1950   Kurt Weill dies (April 3).
1951   *Barefoot in Athens.*
1953   Gertrude Maynard Anderson commits suicide (March 22).
1954   Marries Gilda Oakleaf (June 16). *Bad Seed.*

1955   Buys house (July) in Stamford, Connecticut.
1958   *The Golden Six*. "The Day the Money Stopped."
1959   Dies of stroke in Stamford (February 28).

The Dancing Firefly Years

A CCORDING to Donald Heiney, Maxwell Anderson is "an anomaly in twentieth-century literature," a Romanticist "whose chief contribution to the theatre has been in the virtually obsolete form of verse drama."[1] Heiney might well have added the anomaly of Anderson's making some of this verse drama both an artistic and a commercial success for more than a decade on the Broadway stage. Indeed, several anomalies emerge from the circumstances of Anderson's life and background. He was not born in or around New York City, the birthplace of a surprising number of famous American playwrights; his family contained no artistic or theatrical members of whom record survives, except that his mother painted pictures as a hobby and that an uncle sang on the radio;[2] his youth bordered on poverty; his rearing and most of his formal education took place in the then crude Middle West which was — according to Van Wyck Brooks and despite the interesting opposing evidence by Bernard De Voto — practically a cultural desert; he did not attend Professor G. P. Baker's famous drama class at Harvard, unlike several of his successful contemporaries; and, until he was about thirty-five, he had no intention of making a career out of drama.

I Background and Early Education

As Maxwell Anderson's sister Mrs. Lela A. Chambers admits from her study of the family ancestry, none of the forebears achieved prominence, even though the mother's side of the family included preachers, teachers, musicians, and doctors. Anderson's parents stemmed from families that had arrived in America in the late eighteenth and early nineteenth centuries and settled in Pennsylvania. Considering the fact that Anderson sometimes drew upon his family background for the story material of his dramas, it is at least curious that the great-great-grandfather of the author of *Valley Forge* was a Scotsman in the British Army in America during the Revolutionary War.[3] In this line of descent was William Lincoln (Link) Anderson, Maxwell's father, who in 1885 married nineteen-year-old Perrimela (Premma) Stephenson, who was from the same region of western Pennsylvania.

William Anderson seems to have worked first at lumbering; later, after the birth of his children Ethel Mae and Maxwell, he moved to Andover, Ohio and labored as a fireman on the railroad. Somehow he educated himself,[4] at least to the extent of knowing the Bible well; indeed, he made such a good impression that the congregation at Andover asked him to fill the ministry of the Baptist church. Although he had a remarkable ability for study and remembering, the new preacher showed such a flair for "passionate periods" that he gave his son Maxwell a lifelong aversion to oratory, to all insincere discourse, and to any inclination he himself might have for speechmaking.[5] " 'My father,' " Maxwell Anderson relates, " 'was . . . what you call a good mixer, and a wonderful orator' " — extremely persuasive in the pulpit. " 'But I knew it was all put on.' "[6] A stern and devout man, the Reverend Anderson had planned for Maxwell to pursue an ecclesiastical career, but he was to see him become an agnostic; a member of no church, yet even so an admirer of Christ (*Journey to Jerusalem*); and a deep believer in the spiritual possibilities of man.[7] Lela Chambers, however, is not at all so severe in judging her father and insists that he was also an affectionate and tender man.

Maxwell's mother, Perrimela, was mostly of Scotch-Irish descent, of a lineage somewhat more Romantic and distinguished than her husband's. According to one of the familial accounts, said to be in Lela Chambers' notebooks, the mother had inherited her exotic name Perrimela from an ancestress of noble birth who had escaped from France, perhaps during the French Revolution, with a fortune in jewels and money "sewn into her quilted satin petticoat." This second Perrimela and her sister Emma, the fruit of their father's second marriage, were reared on a farm a half-mile east of the village of Atlantic, Pennsylvania. On this farm, Perrimela's husband built a house for his family; and in this house James Maxwell was born on December 15, 1888, the second child and the eldest son in a flock that was to contain four sons and four daughters.[8]

As the result of the Reverend Anderson's frequent "calls" to successive pastorates, the family moved often in Pennsylvania — perhaps to as many as seventeen hamlets of that state alone[9] — and in Ohio, Iowa, and North Dakota. According to Robert Rice, Maxwell, starting at age thirteen, helped support the family by laboring at "almost every kind of farm work known to man on almost every kind of farm."[10] Because of such frequent moves, his formal education was exceedingly irregular: he finally attended close to a dozen grade schools.[11] By the time he was nine, he was "enjoying every bit of print that came into the house." As his sister Lela remembers, his mastoid infection had kept him from school for a year, had confined him indoors, and had prompted his reading "more than ever." Some of the titles that intrigued Anderson were James Fenimore Cooper's *The Last of the Mohicans*, Robert Louis Stevenson's *Kidnapped*, and A. Conan Doyle's *The Hound of the Baskervilles;* moreover, he must have read Ralph Waldo Emerson's essays well during this time or not much later.

Allan G. Halline, who suspected that Emerson's ideas of the "beneficent tendency" of the universe influenced Anderson (see the final paragraph of Emerson's "The Uses of Poetry"), wrote to the adult Anderson and got the reply that he had indeed grown up on Emerson but was not sure how much that had affected him — possibly a good deal.[12] Emerson's dictum that "Society everywhere is in conspiracy against the manhood of every one of its members" is remarkably apropos to the mind that created such beleaguered individualistic heroes as Alan McClean in *Both Your Houses* and Van Van Dorn in *High Tor*. Very likely Anderson also at this time read Henry David Thoreau, for he was to share with Thoreau a lifelong, profound distrust of "big" government[13] and a lofty individualism that is Thoreauvian if not Emersonian.

In the summer of his tenth year, Anderson returned to Atlantic to the farm of his maternal grandmother, Charlotta, now re-married as a Shepard. There lived also Charlotta's daughter, Emma, who seems to have had, of all of his relatives, the greatest beneficial influence on the development of his imagination. When fall arrived, Maxwell wanted to remain; and, since he was not well, the parents acceded to his wishes and left him to the care of the Shepards — and Emma. "[D]uring the winter days and evenings she [Emma] showed him a side that he had not known," Lela explains. "She was a wonderful story teller of both real and imagined incidents, and she could take the most trivial happening and dress it up into a tale that would challenge her hearer's interest. . . . She told him stories about his ancestors — stories that he remembered so well that in his later life he asked her to write them down for him. . . ." Anderson's dirge "Dust Remembering," written much later, is associated with either Emma or the grandmother. When Lela returned to the farm the next summer, she found that he had acquired from Emma the technique of telling stories, a technique that he delighted to practice upon Lela by the hour back in Harrisburg.

His father bought a second-hand library which contained a set of Charles Dickens novels, one of the standard American poets, histories of France and England, plus some "odds and ends of novels." These books Anderson and the other children "almost read . . . to pieces," but his favorites were the poets. Before or during his fifteenth year, he discovered John Milton and Robert Burns on the parlor book shelves. Later, in a New Hampton, Iowa, drugstore, he bought cheap copies of Percy B. Shelley and the Globe edition of Shakespeare; and, having become enamored of John Keats, he ordered a paperbound set of his poems.[14] The very title of his play *The Eve of St. Mark* suggests a Keatsian influence; and Keats, along with Shakespeare, were always to be his favorites *par excellence*.[15] For him, Shakespeare was Merlin, wizard of language; all other world dramatists were mere players at magic.[16] At some time or other, probably in his youth, he developed a fondness for the poetry of Matthew Arnold, whose classical restraint and melancholy skepticism are so much in keeping with Anderson's own temperament. His tenderly nostalgic letter to the University of North Dakota many years later, on the occasion of its seventy-fifth anniversary, conveys the best single account of his intoxicating adventures among novelists and poets and of his own writing of poetry in secrecy lest the other boys at school jeer at him.[17] The first time that he read any poetry, he knew that he wished to write it, so he told Robert Rice; and he thereafter for many years produced lyrics,[18] though as a group they never matched in quality what was to be his dramatic work.

But Anderson became interested not only in literature but also music; and this interest led to the songs that adorn play after play. While in high school, he learned to read music and to play a violin well enough to join a violin trio; his voice seems to have been melodious, and he belonged to a male quartet. This "singing and reading family," as Lela remembers the Andersons, had an organ and later a piano "which was usually in use whenever any of us children were in the house."[19] Maxwell Anderson's son Alan affirms that "[music] was the one part of his [Maxwell's] father's church that meant a good deal to him." The playwright in adult life played by ear the music of Bach, Beethoven, Mozart, and Chopin on the piano in their home with "devout feeling";[20] his Andre in *Valley Forge* praises Mozart to the skies (Act I, Scene ii). In a telephone interview, Alan related that his father was skillful enough with the piano to compose several songs, at least one of which was used in *Truckline Cafe;*[21] and he also composed the numerous librettos in *Knickerbocker Holiday*, "Ulysses Africanus," *Anne of the Thousand Days*, and *Lost in the Stars*.

II *University of North Dakota and Stanford*

Immediately after Anderson's graduation from high school in Jamestown, North Dakota, he enrolled at the University of North Dakota in the fall of 1908 when he was almost twenty.[22] While at the university, Maxwell impressed others as being rather cynical about men who held great political power, an attitude that would be common in his plays. But this large, broad-shouldered young man had a low, rich voice and was easy-going and "friendly enough when one got to know him yet was not a great mixer — he hardly had time to be," his classmate C. L. Robertson recalls. Somehow, in addition to playing in turn center and right guard on the varsity football team,[23] plus holding part-time jobs, he managed to make excellent grades and to devote some of his spare time to courting his fellow student and future wife, little Margaret C. Haskett, whose ambition stimulated or at least kept pace with his own.

Maxwell and Margaret belonged to the select Sock and Buskin Society that dynamic Professor Frederick H. Koch had formed early in 1910 to promote the study of dramatic literature and the art of the theater; and Koch chose Maxwell as one of his two assistants. Although Professor Koch never claimed that he had "discovered" or trained Anderson as a playwright, he nonetheless must have been a powerful stimulus both in the Sock and Buskin activities and in the two Shakespeare courses that he taught him.[24] Because the teacher's influence was so important in Anderson's life, Koch's academic career is significant. A year after he had arrived at Grand

Forks in 1905 fresh from G. P. Baker and G. L. Kittredge's drama classes at Harvard and had found a play record of nothing but farces and minstrel shows — and a faculty prejudiced against theater, and no theater building either — he had staged R. B. Sheridan's *The Rivals* and had then toured the comedy through little towns of the Dakotas that had never seen a play before.[25] He was himself an outstanding actor both in his classroom readings and on the dramatic stage. Indeed, Professor Koch was an unconventional teacher and a genuine campus "character" of the kind to endear himself to his students for long afterwards, as shown by the many testimonials from Paul Green (*The Lost Colony*), Thomas Wolfe (*The Return of Buck Gavin*), Howard Mumford Jones, and others.[26] Professor Koch was in the best sense a charismatic, enthusiastic, and germinal personality equipped with a rare talent for inspiring original writing.

From Baker, Koch conceived the idea of developing a "school" of regional dramatists — somewhat after the then popular Irish circle of W. B. Yeats, Lady Gregory, and J. M. Synge — that would interpret the rich variety of American experience in dramas worthy of the country's struggles, achievement, and vision.[27] Ironically enough, he was not to begin to realize this dream with the Dakota Playmakers until his most gifted student, Anderson, had graduated and moved on. Koch said about him much later: "He had the feel of the thing [playwriting and theater] in him — long before we wrote plays of our own. . . ."[28] And Anderson, to be sure, was completely sympathetic with his teacher's enterprise once it had started; and he seems to have kept in mind long afterward the desire to write native drama, which Koch sensed when he remarked that Anderson's first Broadway work, "The White Desert" (1923), has its strong folk element and limns the very thing Anderson knew best: his native region, North Dakota's vast and lonely winter plain.[29] The folk element is also strong in Anderson's "Sea-Wife" (1926).

There is no reason to suppose, however, that Koch inspired the first Anderson play of which we have record — the seniors' musical comedy with a Shakespearean title ("Lost Labors Love") written for the senior class when he was a freshman[30] — because teacher and student probably had not met by then. Unquestionably, Professor Koch did have something to do with Anderson's second seniors' musical comedy, "The Masque of Pedagogues," penned during his third and final year, because Koch is directly though gently lampooned in the skit.[31] In this piece of juvenilia we find already the

Elizabethan devices of verse dialogue and songs that later figure in Anderson's mature history plays about Queen Elizabeth, Mary of Scotland, and Anne Boleyn.

Not surprisingly, Anderson's second musical comedy contains five references to Shakespeare and two to Keats. Its action is patently a take-off on Christopher Marlowe's *Doctor Faustus* in that Lucifer visits errant scholars at the University of North Dakota and makes a bargain with them for some wicked knowledge: from their fiendish assignments and tests, he is to pick up some tips for new kinds of tortures in hell! Obviously "The Masque of Pedagogues" is hardly the play that shows the influence of Koch at his best; it is mainly a revelation of some of Anderson's abiding literary interests wrapped up as a clever bagatelle for the cedar chest of school memories. Still, it serves as a beginning in the craft of writing.[32] It is to be noticed that two of his mature plays also carry *masque* in their titles: *The Masque of Kings* and "The Masque of Queens." Very possibly, if Koch had not been around, Anderson might not have tried stagecraft again so soon. A more important thought still is that if Anderson had only been in one of the classes starting with 1914, when Koch first began making native plays, he might have begun his professional career in the theater many years earlier than he did.[33]

Anderson took a total of eight courses from another memorable figure, Professor Gottfried Hult, "a learned and loveable man"[34] and a poet in his own right; and these courses included Greek language, literature, archaeology, and philosophy, in all of which the student showed a strong interest.[35] Many years later, he was to challenge in his *Barefoot in Athens* the interpretation of Socrates' character that he had learned under Hult. He completed two courses in history under the then nationally known Orin G. Libby; and there is little doubt, judging from Libby's prominence in the skit previously described, that he made a strong impression on the lad who would one day pen some famous history plays.

Anderson was able to graduate in three years: he later confessed that he finished early because he was stuffed with information about English literature,[36] some of which could have contributed to his four mature dramas on the English Renaissance. Soon after graduation in 1911, he married Miss Haskett, who seems to have made him a devoted and congenial wife.[37] She bore him three sons, namely Quentin Maxwell, Alan Haskett, and Terence, in that order.[38] Alan would one day direct some of his father's plays.

During the first two years after leaving Grand Forks, Anderson acted as a principal[39] and also taught English in a high school in Minnewaukan, North Dakota. At this time, when the passions of the country were stirred because of the possibility of America's involvement in World War I, he bravely took an antiwar stance;[40] he "talked pacifism" to his students, thereby incurring the wrath of the school board, which promptly ended his contract.[41] His antiwar sentiment survived and was one day expressed in *What Price Glory*. The fall of 1913 saw him living at Palo Alto, California and taking courses at Stanford University. Contrary to some published accounts, he was never a regular teacher at this school; instead, he held a temporary position as "assistant" (probably like today's graduate assistant). In 1914 he received his master's degree in English after writing a thesis that testified to his continuing fascination with the Olympian of playwrights: it bore the title "Immortality in the Plays and Sonnets of Shakespeare."[42]

III   *Casting about for a Career*

Anderson spent the following three years teaching at Polytechnic High School in San Francisco,[43] and he may have moonlighted by furnishing items for the San Francisco *Bulletin*.[44] In 1916, he published a half-dozen juvenilia in *A Stanford Book of Verse*,[45] and he soon furnished verse for national journals, such as *The New Republic*. Although he does not seem to have enjoyed teaching,[46] he nevertheless procured the headship of the English Department at Whittier College; perhaps he believed that a pacifist would feel quite at home among the Quakers who were and are such reputed advocates of nonviolence. How wrong he was to be! Whittier College was at the time of Anderson's arrival in late 1917 controlled rigidly by a board of conservative and mostly Quaker trustees who, if typical of American Friends then, were most likely divided in their support of compulsory military service and, moreover, were subject to the pressures of war hysteria from the surrounding community.[47] The courses Anderson scheduled were innocuous enough; and, from what is known, the students were at least satisfied with what they then learned under the gentle but beetle-browed "Bolshevik" (which then meant a radical, not a Communist).[48] Morris Kimber, a Whittier professor, has recalled his brother Thomas' immense enthusiasm about his work under Anderson, while Raymond C. Hunnicutt, who took playwriting under him, has averred that he still has some of the plays written for the course.[49]

When Anderson publicly defended the right of a draft-resisting student, Arthur Camp, to publish in the *Quaker Campus* a statement about his convictions,[50] he brought pressure upon himself from the community, according to Dr. Charles Cooper in his history of Whittier College. Although the school dean tried to mediate and to get the idealistic new teacher to retract, Anderson adamantly refused to accommodate himself to the prevailing intolerance — just as several of his mature dramas (*Gods of the Lightning*, *Winterset*, *Wingless Victory*, and *Lost in the Stars*) oppose intolerance. Somewhat about this time, the gentle professor won still more disfavor at Whittier by reading a martial poem entitled "A Prayer before Battle" to a class of his and by then observing aloud "that it would be most unfortunate if the other side [the Germans] were praying in a similar fashion for victory and the annihilation of its enemy, since Heaven might then be in danger of becoming confused." Within a week, the school discharged him;[51] and Anderson seems to have gone next to San Francisco where, in July, he was to occupy an editorial slot on the *Bulletin*.[52]

Cooper assures us that Anderson was not bitter about his treatment at Whittier, at least by the time of World War II when he allowed the college to stage one of his plays.[53] But bitter or not, the playwright showed little kindness for Quakers in his dramas: in *Valley Forge*, the hungry soldier Alcock in Washington's army sneers at how a Quaker would prefer to sell hogs to the British forces rather than serve the cause of freedom (Act I, Scene i); in *Knickerbocker Holiday*, the councilman Tienhoven thinks it more festive to hang a Quaker than a Baptist because the former takes a longer time dying (Act I).[54] Though Anderson was never again a member of academe, his experience there could have helped imbue his characteristic dramas with a certain lofty seriousness, a tolerant and balanced skepticism, a profound and yet Romantic feeling for the sweep of human history, and a scholar's fondness for absorbing into his own literary creations the fragrance of bygone vogues and traditions.

The courage and individualism that were to mark Anderson's dramas began to appear quite early in his newspaper work. Indeed, his *Bulletin* job ended promptly after he submitted an editorial that declared Germany would find it impossible to reimburse all of the Allies for the war costs. Luckily — for there were two young children in the family now — he obtained a copy-desk job right away on the rival *Chronicle*. Soon Alvin Johnson invited him to become an editor on *The New Republic;* and so, with money borrowed from two spinsters in the neighborhood (and re-paid from the first royalties of *What Price Glory*), he traveled to New York and eventual fortune.[55] Perhaps the kindness of those spinsters found its way somehow into the tender affection with which he treats numerous penny-plain souls in his dramas.

Johnson had him in mind for writing liberal editorials; but, upon discovering that he had instead hired a radical, he shifted Anderson to book reviews. After six months the latter moved to the New York *Globe* paper. About this time he joined a number of artists in originating the poetry magazine *The Measure*, in which he printed some of his own poems. His brilliant *Globe* editorials began to attract the attention of the rival *World* whose agent talked him into shifting to that paper; still, since he was not happy there for long,[56] he grew bored, sufficiently so to try his hand at serious playwriting; and the play underway was "White Desert."[57]

Anderson's restless and unsatisfying years of newspaper experience did have at least three agreeable effects upon his subsequent dramatic development: (1) Editorial writing, despite all its hazards and distractions for the creative mind that looks for things of permanent value and interest in the kaleidoscopic whirl of daily events, helped train him to avoid the trivial and to focus on the larger social and political forces. (2) Journalism acquainted him with various levels of public taste and how to satisfy that taste — for good or ill. (3) And, as Anderson told Robert Rice, newspaper work accustomed him to write rapidly; whether writing or re-writing plays, all of it was done rapidly.[58]

IV   *On South Mountain Road*

For most of his creative career Anderson was to live around and sometimes in New York City. In 1919, he rented a house in Grand-View-on-the-Hudson; the next year, he lived in Greenwich Village; the year afterward, he bought and moved into a small, two-storied, old farmhouse located on thirty acres of wilderness land in New City. Except for winters in New York City, he lived for the next ten years in this plain dwelling alongside the unpaved South Mountain Road. The site had both isolation and rustic beauty: Anderson's attic study looked down a spectacular waterfall of "unimaginable beauty" that fell through "a magnificent redstone ravine with caves once used by Indians who left behind some of their artifacts."[59] Bare and simple, the house boasted no electricity, telephone, running water, or flush toilet; but it was the very kind of Spartan arrangement that his hero Van Dorn in *High Tor* would have relished.

Anderson's neighbors in New City included a few young writers, painters, sculptors, and musicians, including Carroll French; the musician Harold Hickerson with whom Anderson was to collaborate on *Gods of the Lightning* (1928); and the future star of *Winterset* (1935), Burgess Meredith, who was attracted to and made famous by the playwright with whom he had many walks and conversations.[60] Among all the artists through the years, Anderson's greatest friend was the opera and musical composer Kurt Weill. Because Kurt Weill's music had been condemned by the philistine bootlickers of Hitler, he had left Germany in 1933 and had soon established residence on South Mountain Road in order to be near the dramaturgist Anderson. Weill eventually wrote scores for several of his friend's plays; and his actress-wife Lotte Lenya performed in Anderson's *Candle in the Wind* and in his *Barefoot in Athens*. Another friend and neighbor was the diminutive actress Helen Hayes who starred in his *Mary of Scotland* (1933) and in *Candle in the Wind* (1941). So much that was close and dear to Maxwell Anderson was during his thirty years of living in New City: the formative effects upon his life and work must have been both numerous and profound.

After Anderson's first wife died of a stroke in 1931, he married again, this time to the young, Canadian-born actress Gertrude (Mab) Maynard; and he commissioned his artist friend Henry Varnum Poor — whose picture of nearby High Tor, called "Grey Dawn," hangs in the Metropolitan Museum of Art — to design another but far more expensive house for him in the neighborhood.[61] While living in this baronial house, he discovered, to his immense shock, that Mab was being unfaithful; and, as a result, he rejected her violently, resisted his friends' attempts to effect a reconciliation, and left her to suffer there in lonely remorse. Somehow, he could not muster the husbandly forgiveness that he had his fictional hero practice in a similar crisis in *Truckline Cafe* (1946).

Beyond help from friends who tried to console her, she finally gave up and took her own life in 1953.[62] Soon he married a third time, to Gilda Oakleaf, and bought an expensive house at 141 Downes Avenue in Stamford, Connecticut, which was to be his home for the rest of his life.[63]

V *White Desert and Other Landscapes*

Surprisingly, Alan Anderson has related that his father as a young man wanted more than anything else to compose not drama but *poetry* for a living![64] Despite Maxwell Anderson's playwriting successes at the university, and his tutelage under the inspiring Professor Koch, the evidence shows that before he traveled east to New York City he never seriously felt that drama was his proper medium. Almost certainly the change of goals came in large measure from his sudden proximity to the bustling, commercial stage of Broadway where fame and fortune lured in the myriad lights of theater marquees and enticed him to re-evaluate his career. Nevertheless, throughout Anderson's young manhood, when he was growing increasingly dissatisfied with teaching and journalism, theater was one of the careers in which he was *not* interested.[65] Once this desire was born, however, his chief motivation for theatrical writing stemmed at first from money — and the motivation never completely left him. "It occurred to me," Anderson remarks in his essay "A Confession" that was published in the *New York Times*, December 5, 1954, "that I might combine the desire to make money with my aspiration to be a poet . . . ." His subsequent career can be interpreted, therefore, as that of one who wanted dearly to make a living by poetry; but, failing at this and seeing how apparently easy it is to get rich at the box office, he turned to drama and consoled himself periodically by originating verse drama — the glorious Andersonian compromise.

The turning point occurred in 1922 while Anderson was still on the staff of the *World*, for his nearest neighbor at New City was a young dramatist whose first play had won from the Theatre Guild an advance of five hundred dollars, a sum that dazzled the restive journalist. When Anderson heard the play read aloud one evening, he told himself that, if such a flabby item could earn so much money, he too should try. Following a bad start, he chanced to recall a story that his wife had once told him about her parents' struggles on a North Dakota mining claim; and from this story grew the verse play "White Desert."[66] He chose poetry as his medium because, he said, he was "weary" of prose plays that "never lifted from the ground."[67] Nevertheless, he had made a bold and risky choice because verse dramas were and still are distressingly hard to market. He showed his experiment to Laurence Stallings, at that time a book reviewer on the *World*, who passed it to another colleague, Deems Taylor, friend of the Broadway producer Brock Pemberton. Anderson got his five hundred dollars advance; Pemberton staged "White Desert" on October 18, 1923; and the whole enterprise promptly failed.[68]

With actor George Abbott, Anderson next wrote "A Holy Terror," which was also far from being a success on the boards. But with his next co-author, Stallings, his play *What Price Glory* quickly became a box office bonanza.[69] On that opening night in 1924, Anderson had good reason to feel, as he watched the playgoers *stand up in their seats and cheer*,[70] that he had found at last his true profession. His future friend and business partner Robert E. Sherwood attended one of *Glory*'s performances; and, seeing the audience rise up and applaud so warmly, he decided then and there that he himself had to become a playwright.[71]

In 1924, Anderson wrote "Sea-Wife," which has never been professionally staged. The next year, he collaborated twice more with Stallings: they produced the swashbuckling historical romance *First Flight*, which portrayed the youthful dueling lover Andrew Jackson, and also *The Buccaneer*, which dealt with pirate Captain Henry Morgan; but neither play was a success on the stage. That same year, Anderson alone wrote *Outside Looking In*, a rather aimless study of social injustice — a hobo's rivalry for supremacy and control of a girl — which was based on the novel *Beggars of Life* by Jim Tully. Also issued in 1925 was Anderson's collection of poetry entitled *You Who Have Dreams*. Thus in a four-year span at the opening of his career — 1923 to 1926 — he essayed several, but by no means all, of the genres that were to be characteristic of him: poetic tragedy, war play, historical romance, social problem play, and poetic fantasy.

The year 1927 brought a stage success and also a relative failure in two studies of modern love and marriage: the long-running *Saturday's Children* is a domestic problem play exploring the economic basis of happiness among newlyweds; and "Gypsy," acted that fall but never published, is in some ways ominously prophetic of the horror to occur in Anderson's second marriage, for this play concerns a girl with bad heredity (mother a nymphomaniac) and worse upbringing who marries against her better judgment, cuckolds her husband, and then kills herself.[72] Both stories are sympathetically told, but neither of these ventures into literary Naturalism constitutes outstanding drama; and the same is true of *Gods of the Lightning* (1928), written with Harold Hickerson.

The 1920's in the American theater had belonged to Eugene O'Neill; the 1930's were by and large Maxwell Anderson's. *Elizabeth the Queen* opened the decade as the first of three Tudor dramas for which he has been justly acclaimed. But two years later he brought out the weak *Night over Taos* (Conchita acted by his future wife Gertrude Maynard);[73] this play has interested very few critics and clearly belongs among his lesser credits. Plays continued to pour forth: *Both Your Houses* and *Mary of Scotland* (both 1933); *Valley Forge* (1934); *Winterset* (1935); and *The Wingless Victory* (1936). Then 1937 led in *High Tor*, *The Masque of Kings*, *The Star-Wagon*, and *The Feast of Ortolans* (a radio piece aired by the National Broadcasting Company. The Russian Revolution that he had so joyously hailed in his poem "Sic Semper" back in 1917,[74] he showed as betrayed in his 1938 one-act *Second Overture*.[75] Also in 1938 came the hilarious musical comedy *Knickerbocker Holiday*, his first collaborative effort with Kurt Weill. The next year, 1939, he brought out one of his more impressive tragedies, *Key Largo*. When Anderson's story of the boy-Christ, *Journey to Jerusalem* (1940), was produced, it became one of his all-round failures, despite the noblest of intentions; he had decided to ignore the legal objections to its presentation — a New York State law forebade the depiction of the deity in the theater — and to go ahead and stage the work because, as Laurence Avery has suggested, of "the importance he attached to the problem of faith in a world threatened by Hitler."[76] *The Miracle of the Danube*, a propagandist one-act that was broadcast early in 1941 over the Columbia Broadcasting System radio, illustrated for Americans the danger of the widening war and the meaning of freedom. In the same year, *Candle in the Wind* told about the Nazi invasion of France: an even clearer warning to the Western democracies. Still another one-act item of radio propaganda was *Your Navy*, designed to gird America for war mobilization;[77] likewise, his patriotic bagatelle *Letter to Jackie* edified war-production workers as part of the Lunchtime Follies program of the Stage Door Canteen.

Unquestionably his best drama of the war proved to be *The Eve of St. Mark* (1942). In his private life during world War II, patriot Anderson worked as co-ordinator of civil defense and had charge of airplane spotters in his district; in the company of Kurt Weill, he watched for planes one night a week.[78] The last of his war plays was *Storm Operation* (1944), a huge, all-round disappointment.

In the year after the war ended, *Truckline Cafe* and *Joan of Lorraine* appeared; and two years later, his last story of English court intrigue, *Anne of the Thousand Days*. In an altogether different vein ran the operatic *Lost in the Stars* which was drawn from Alan Paton's novel *Cry, the Beloved Country*; and this work was Anderson's final produced collaboration with Kurt Weill, who died soon after on April 3, 1950. For the humanitarian contribution of *Lost in the Stars*, Anderson received the Brotherhood Award of the National Conference of Christians and Jews. Partly the result of, or merely coincidental with, the death of his best friend and collaborator, something vital disappeared from Anderson the creative artist, who was then in his sixties, for, during the next several years, little that he wrote caught either critical approval or public fancy.

Barefoot in Athens (1951), about Socrates, died quickly from its own built-in hemlock; but three years later some vitality returned to Anderson when he adapted the novel *The Bad Seed* by William March into an enormously popular and satisfying stage play. Always willing, too willing, to undertake motion picture scriptwriting and other such chores to support his then extravagant scale of living, he also dramatized Charles Dickens' *Christmas Carol* for Columbia Broadcasting System television. *The Golden Six* and "The Day the Money Stopped," this last an adaptation of a comic novel by Brendon Gill, were the final plays that Anderson saw produced, and both of them foundered almost immediately the year before he passed away.

VI *Dramatic Rules and Applications*

In 1939, Maxwell Anderson turned critic in *The Essence of Tragedy and Other Footnotes and Papers*, in the leading essay of which he enunciated the first systematic theory of tragedy yet to arise from an American dramatist; and, save for the later essay "Tragedy and the Common Man" by Arthur Miller, it is the only one to date. His second book of criticism, *Off Broadway Essays about the Theatre*, reached print in 1947. His dramatic theory — studied in depth by Allan G. Halline, Mabel D. Bailey, and Arthur M. Sampley,[79] among others — is located mainly in the essays in these two books. There is good reason to believe that his theory of tragedy, first expounded in January, 1938, was already complete by July 14, 1933, the date that he finished the first play to follow it obediently, *Mary of Scotland*.[80] Since he worked out the other parts of his dramatic theory at about the same time, he was theorizing after the fact (as is common practice with artists) and was seemingly justifying his own method.

We should keep in mind that Anderson was an unashamed traditionalist in his views about the nature and function of the playwright as well as about certain elements in the creation of drama. To dismiss him as unoriginal, as some have done, is to treat him unfairly; for he made no claim at all to originality when he offered his re-discoveries of the principles he had found in the actual practice of successful dramatists through the ages, notably the Greeks, Shakespeare, other Renaissance figures, and certain moderns. As for the writer himself, Anderson held with Aristotle that the tragedian must be a poet because the heightening of the effect of true tragedy, its appeal to emotions, absolutely demands poetry. To him, prose seemed the language for information; poetry, the language for emotion. Although Anderson admitted that prose could be forced to convey emotion, as in works by Synge and O'Casey where unfamiliar rhythms of speech are used, he considered the usual prose of the theater to be inarticulate.[81] He was modest enough to believe, however, that he himself was not the great poet needed to create tragedy for our age.

But, being more than just a poet, the dramatist had to be a prophet in a special sense and an "interpreter of the racial dream." To accomplish such a mission, the dramatist would have to ignore the clod that man is and concentrate on the god man could become; in actual stagecraft, however, insofar as we can draw our examples from Anderson's own practice, it meant sometimes that the artist would present the clod to so disgust man that he, ashamed and disgusted, might resolve to be noble. The legislator-villains in *Both Your Houses* are excellent examples of this type. To Anderson, man was certain to change; and what he would become would be conditioned by what he dreamed and desired. The playwright, therefore, held a serious, even holy, responsibility; the theater in which he functioned was to be dedicated to the exaltation of man's spirit;[82] indeed, the playwright, being something of a prophet, so believed in the worthwhileness of the human race that he forecast its gradual growth in wisdom.[83] As Halline has remarked with justice, Anderson's vision of the artist as a prophet of an improved race resembles R. W. Emerson's concept of the poet as mankind's "sayer";[84] therefore, the dramatist is not merely a poet but also a cosmic philosopher — as witness some of d'Alcala's inspiring dialogue in Act II of *Key Largo*. As a result, Anderson refused to place his art in the service of (as Max Eastman wanted and worded it) "[a] *practical scientific* . . . effort to solve the problems of life on this planet" simply because poetry is quite unsuited for that business: furthermore, utilitarian needs do not evoke any poetry worth the name.[85] Anderson's drama, for the most part, differs sharply from the left-wing social commentary characteristic of the 1930's. Inasmuch as he is referring in the foregoing rationale to *dramatic* poetry only, we have to discount the fact that Lucretius once wrote some scientific verses (*De Rerum Natura*) that have survived the ages.

After some bitter failures in theater, Anderson made a search for workable principles or rules of playwriting that might assure him of more than accidental success with his dramas; accordingly, he re-read Aristotle's *Poetics* and found that the recognition scene described there — though usually an artificial device, such as the penetration of a disguise or hidden identity — was something the Greeks employed most convincingly in some of their finest plays. Moreover, the device is still present in the plays of Shakespeare and of the moderns, but it is more difficult to find and subtler. Thus by pragmatic rather than theoretical means, Anderson formulated in due course his own version of the recognition scene — a step in the direction of what Gassner terms "Romantic Aristotelianism."[86] As Anderson saw it, the hero in a modern play almost always discovers something in himself or in his environment about which he had been unaware or had imperfectly understood. A play had to show the chief character make such a discovery — one that would deeply affect his thought and emotions and completely change his conduct. To Anderson, this crisis occurs near the end of Act II in a three-act play and usually happens near the end of Act III in a five-act play.[87] By examination of successful plays of the past, he discovered a group of rules that governed serious drama, especially tragedy, by which the artist had to abide:

1. The play deals with the heart or mind of a person, not mainly with external events.
2. The story must consist of a conflict inside a single human being between good and evil, and such categories are defined according to the audience's judgment.
3. The protagonist, representative of the forces of good, must win; if he has represented evil, he must be defeated by the good and realize the fact.
4. The protagonist, who must emerge at the end of the play as more admirable than at the beginning, must not be perfect.
5. The protagonist has to be exceptional; or, if he is a man from the street, he must epitomize qualities of excellence that the audience is able to admire.
6. Excellence on the stage must ever be moral excellence.
7. A healthy moral atmosphere must prevail in the play; evil must not triumph.
8. The theater audience admires these human qualities on the stage: woman's passionate faith and fidelity, man's strength of conviction and positive character; the audience especially resents these qualities: woman's infidelity, man's cowardice and refusal to fight for a belief.[88]

To Anderson, the theme of tragedy meant a victory snatched from defeat at that moment when man is confronted with annihilation. In the last act of the play, the hero goes simultaneously to a spiritual enlightenment and to his death; and the message left is that mankind is worthier than it thinks it is[89] — precisely the view that Emerson iterated so eloquently in "Self-Reliance" and in other essays. In most of the dramas, especially from the 1930's onward, there definitely is some kind of idea to be conveyed, quite aside from mere entertainment; for Anderson was committed to the old Romantic belief, shared by some of his contemporary playwrights, that the form of a play is only a convenient means with which to communicate content. In "The Essence of Tragedy" he defines a play as being practically always an effort to recapture for the theater the artist's vision (p.5). This message, deeply rooted in the work, is expressed only in symbols; and it cannot be reduced to a plain statement.[90] The reader or audience, not the playwright, has the responsibility, therefore, for interpreting the meaning of the drama. Some of the more obvious symbols found in Anderson's plays include the mountain and the steam shovel in *High Tor*, and the bridge in *Winterset*.

His plays of the 1920's showed him trying out various types of subject matter and treatment as he groped toward some useful formulation of dramaturgical principles; sometimes he created an artistically successful play long before the formulation was complete, as in *What Price Glory*; in only two of the completed plays did he use poetry; and in only one of these, "White Desert," did he even attempt tragedy. Probably his artistic and commercial triumph with the transitional *Elizabeth the Queen* (1930), which employed most but not all of his dramatic theories, encouraged him to develop and apply the theories further: he did so starting with *Mary of Scotland* (1933) and used them often in his richly varied corpus. But the strict application of the theories did not guarantee success; and when success did arrive, it was sometimes owing to causes quite beyond the mere application of rules, as we shall see later. Some of his best realized plays, e.g., *Anne of the Thousand Days*, *Bad Seed*, and *High Tor*, violate one or more of the forementioned rules — the first two plays, rule seven; the last one, rule three. But the rules did help him.

Gerald Rabkin has summarized cogently what Anderson did in challenging the prosaic leftist stage of the 1930's with his effort to rejuvenate drama, including tragedy, by means of poetic treatment: "Anderson's effort, then, represents a conscious attempt to re-emphasize the role of individual heroics in a world — and in a theater — in which the individual seemed to exist only as a representative of larger social forces. In the world of Anderson's dramatic imagination, the protagonist is invariably a man or woman . . . fighting a losing battle against hostile — usually evil — social forces."[91] The reader can see in Rabkin's statement why rule three is often in danger of being violated.

The poetry of Anderson's plays is usually an unobtrusive, irregular kind of blank verse. He chose iambic pentameter because, as he told one correspondent, it unites intensity and loftiness with the least of artificiality; moreover, such poetry is unlike free verse which resembles complicated and inflated prose.[92] In Anderson's dramas, this blank verse is sometimes admirably suited to convey the rhythms of today's speech and yet distill a literary flavor. In the year before his death, he was bitter because his poetic dramas had not been received as well as they might have been; and he also asserted that, since we live in an age of prose, his verse plays could have been presented in prose without making any difference to anyone — except himself.[93] Of course, he was far too pessimistic in this assessment.

VII *Secrets of the Cabin*

Knowing Maxwell Anderson's writing habits and general method of composition might enable us to understand better not merely the artist himself but also his art. Some published accounts tell of his one-room cabin study situated in the woods about a half-mile back of his new house on South Mountain Road. In the spring, he waded there through freshets; in winter, he dug a path through snow drifts. The independence suggested by the isolation of the cabin was matched by the honesty of the plain and functional furnishings inside, such as the "dumpy, black-iron stove" that looked "like Napoleon after Waterloo, sulking in a corner." Sedgwick discloses that Anderson's library in the cabin contained works by and about Shakespeare, ancient Greek plays, one or more titles by Aristotle (almost assuredly the *Poetics*), essays, biographies, and histories.[94] But few, if any, novels — he rarely read them.[95]

We can discount the rumor spread by Robert Rice that Anderson slept much of the day on the cabin bed,[96] and we can do so not merely because Alan Anderson has denied it but because the father was such a prolific worker. When in the thick of a drama, he typically rose early at the house and worked throughout the day without a break except for lunch. "He didn't usually write in the evening," Alan Anderson recalls, "unless he was under great pressure to get something ready for a rehearsal or if he had been interrupted during the day or if he simply felt compelled to 'work on the next scene.' " Anderson was particularly eager to be at his desk when it started raining, for he thrilled at being near and hearing the sounds of water: "He drove everyone else mad," Alan tells in amazement, "because he insisted that his favorite weather was RAIN!"

In the early years, when Maxwell Anderson was working in the old farmhouse attic that overlooked the falls and the gorge, the low, gushing sound of the cataract penetrated even the closed windows to furnish a soothing background for his writing; later, when he moved to the new house nearby, the cabin behind it was nestled alongside a spring and its brook which, however, were not vocal and inspiring enough for his pleasure. He consequently mounted on the roof a water sprinkler system which he could turn on to keep the cabin damp and cool in the heat of summer! And, late in life, after he had migrated to Shaippan Point in Stamford, there roared just outside his living room windows the breakers of Long Island Sound. Maurice Zolotow records the actress Lynn Fontanne as saying that Anderson, by his own confession, was delayed in re-writing *Elizabeth the Queen* because he "could only write when it rained" — luckily, a heavy rainstorm came in Baltimore at that time and enabled him there to complete the re-writing needed for the play's success.[97] We can find this mysterious water symbol operating *within* his plays, too: *Mary of Scotland, Winterset,* and *High Tor* all have rain or sleet in them; and not only do these same three plays use one or more settings adjacent to a large body of water, but so do "Sea-Wife," *The Wingless Victory, Key Largo, The Miracle of the Danube, The Eve of St. Mark,* and *Storm Operation.*

Among the dramatists that he admiringly read, or continued to read, during his professional years were of course Shakespeare, Sophocles (he thought one particular production of *Oedipus Rex* his most affecting experience in all of theater),[98] Christopher Marlowe *(Doctor Faustus),* Johann W. Goethe, Jean Molière, Henrik Ibsen, Ferenc Molnar *(Liliom),* Marc Connelly *(Green Pastures),* Sidney Howard *(They Knew What They Wanted),* Robert E. Sherwood *(Abe Lincoln in Illinois),* G. B. Shaw (whom he praises in the essay "St. Bernard"), Sean O'Casey *(Plough and the Stars* — Anderson's favorite among contemporary plays),[99] J. M. Synge, and Eugene O'Neill — though he was unable to bear sitting through a performance of *The Iceman Cometh,*[100] whose depressing Nihilism was antithetical to Anderson's rather hopeful temper in the post-1939 years. However, he felt that the last four writers, the best of the moderns, were all inferior to the great playwrights of the past for the reason that, with the exception of O'Casey, none of them were poets.[101] Obviously, his tastes were conditioned somewhat by his poetic theory, and maybe vice versa.

Anderson's period of *textual* collaborations ended in 1928, no doubt because so few of them, only *What Price Glory,* had struck fire, and because he had reached by then a high degree of independence as an artist. However, his musical collaborations started in the late 1930's with Weill — "the only indisputable genius" he had ever known, he said[102] — whose melodies suited Anderson's librettos perfectly. From early to late Anderson sometimes chose a novel for adaptation; of the novels thus used, only two became successful artistically or commercially on the stage. In those plays which were neither adaptations nor collaborations, he evidently never employed anyone else to do research for him, as we can see in his letter of refusal to Mrs. Keehn, who had offered her assistance.[103]

Other than novels, his chief sources of stories and settings were actual experiences of people he knew or had heard about; but he also used biographies and histories which gave him material for plays about famous personalities from Greek, Roman, Elizabethan, European, Mexican, and early American eras. Avery, having studied the diaries — see "The Maxwell Anderson Papers" (p. 26) — tells us that Anderson read "a good deal of history" to prepare for the historical dramas.

Sometimes Anderson had particular actors in mind for the roles he wanted to create; sometimes he finished the plays first, then decided upon the actors, and actively sought to secure them. This common practice among the members of The Playwrights' Producing Company might help account for John Gassner's essentially erroneous conclusion that Anderson was mainly a practical man of the theater and only secondarily a poet and tragedian.[104] In a letter to Paul Muni, we learn that the dramatist had proposed to him a play about Napoleon; but, when Muni demurred, Anderson sought a subject that would interest the actor. The next year, 1939, he outlined to Paul Robeson an unwritten musical entitled "Aeneas Africanus" (later re-titled "Ulysses Africanus") in which he wanted him to act.[105] After Anderson had finished his *Joan of Lorraine* script, he made a special trip to Hollywood to sign a contract with Ingrid Bergman who was to play the title role.[106] In 1949, he planned for Rex Harrison to star in the as yet unwritten "Adam, Lilith and Eve." Next year, Anderson's old-time friend Burgess Meredith, whom he had long before selected as the lead in both *High Tor* and *The Star-Wagon*, insisted that he frame a play around the adventurer T. E. Lawrence, whose stage enactment would mean a role for the versatile Meredith; although Anderson attempted to write such a play, he abandoned the project. In the fall of that year, 1950, Anderson was still trying to develop dramas around star players; for he was planning "Cytherea" as a vehicle for Helen Hayes.[107]

From available evidence, Anderson rarely if ever made notes for a given play.[108] His typical method of composition that he started in the 1930's required that, after finding his characters and subject, he early decide on the recognition scene (the hero's discovery of something in himself or in his environment about which he had been unaware or had imperfectly understood). Then he sketched briefly the play divisions and proceeded to write the script neatly by hand in a large ledger of one hundred and fifty to three hundred pages. Such a script, not exceeding one hundred pages, went through three stages of revision; and each stage of revision is clearly visible in the surviving manuscripts.[109] At this juncture, he took the script to his wife for typing, or, more commonly, to a secretary at The Playwrights' Producing Company at 630 Fifth Avenue, New York City. This company — a twentieth-century "Pleiad" organized in the spring of 1938 by Maxwell Anderson, Sidney Howard, S. N. Behrman, Robert E. Sherwood, and Elmer Rice — was a unique organization of playwrights interested in producing their own plays with the minimum of restrictions. It operated harmoniously for twenty-two years and gave to its several members incalculable advantages from the close association of like-minded artists.[110]

The typescript, sent back to Anderson's cabin, passed through two more revisions, ones which seem to have bored him. By his own admission, as we noted earlier, he wrote rapidly; but, lest we conclude that he did not revise enough, Avery assures us that the dramas revised the most extensively, such as *Candle in the Wind*, are with few exceptions the poorest ones. The final copy — before rehearsals that usually produced changes rarely suited to his taste — represented the final authoritative text; consequently, it was the one published[111] by, for instance, the Anderson House Publishing Company in which he shared a joint partnership with his brother Kenneth, the manager of the business transactions.

VIII *First Night, Jukes Family, and Hollywood*

During the weeks of rehearsal, this big, shy, gentle man with the thin, reddish mustache, big ears, high forehead, and grave face could be seen in one of the New York City theaters; he was present only because the director might want one of the scenes adjusted or a line re-written that was not playing well. When he talked, it was about serious matters, just as his plays often were. "He was not happy with gossip, idle chatter . . . ," Alan Anderson informs us. When Maxwell Anderson attended one of his own premieres, he kept himself aloof, inconspicuous; and, after the showing, he slipped away unobtrusively, avoiding the bright cafe society. Unless some business of The Playwrights' Producing Company drew him to town, he was not to be seen again on the Great White Way until he had finished his next work.[112]

During his flush 1930's, Anderson had no serious quarrel with Broadway drama critics about the manner in which they handled his work.[113] But he had changed his mind by 1942 and had begun a private war on the circle of newspaper critics. Accordingly, when he permitted the National Theatre Conference to tour *The Eve of St. Mark* around the country before its Broadway showing, he stipulated that the production was to be kept sufficiently away from the city so that the New York critics could not attend and have the opportunity to shoot it down before the general public could judge the play for itself.[114] As a believer in a democratic theater, he put his faith wholeheartedly in the tastes of the public; moreover, he knew that, throughout centuries of literature, the critics had almost always been badly mistaken about the worth of contemporary writers until gradually the public had corrected them.[115] One reason that Anderson assigned first importance to the general public is that he felt his drama had to have more or less immediate acceptance on the stage in order to survive because, as he said, no writer in the history of the theater ever left behind a quantity of unappreciated material which gradually achieved recognition; hence, as Anderson stated in "Poetry in the Theatre," the dramatist had to aim for immediate acceptance (p. 4). What he fails to say is that this method might court temporary popularity rather than lasting respect, a circumstance unfortunately true of some of his own work. No doubt he was thinking of the example of Molière, after whose career he seems to have patterned his own; for Anderson wrote in "A Confession" that, when Molière failed with one type of play, he then wrote a different one, even a lightweight musical, to please the theater; that Molière always aimed at quality as well as commercial success; and that he knew that a play had to win applause right away if it were to last the ages.

Anderson was convinced that the newspaper critics, whom he described as blasé, pained souls who attended the theater merely out of duty, wielded too much power over any drama staged in New York City; for their smile practically assured a box-office bonanza; their frown, the loss of a fortune. A "no" from them would altogether prevent the public from exercising its own more important functions, which presumably amount to some kind of implicit critical evaluation linked with the desire and the ability to transmit a deserving play to future generations. Aside from the expenditure in talent and time on the part of the dramatist in preparing a drama, the financial gamble that was necessary for a production had increased. In the 1923–27 era, someone could actually stage a regular play in New York City for as little as ten thousand dollars;[116] by 1938, the figure had soared to about twenty-five thousand dollars, the amount originally set then by The Playwrights' Producing Company as reasonable for a production, although the Company had weakened that year and had lavished sixty thousand dollars on the musical *Knickerbocker Holiday;*[117] by 1948, a play, minus scenery, cost from sixty thousand to seventy thousand dollars;[118] and, in the next decade, thanks to continuing inflation and union demands, the costs skyrocketed so that, by the end of Anderson's career, producers commonly spent one hundred thousand dollars on a one-set play that required a modest-sized cast, and from three hundred to five hundred thousand dollars on a musical. And, with this rise in cost, the total number of new productions each season diminished because television[119] and motion pictures were luring audiences away from the theater. Consequently, Anderson had ample cause in the 1940's for apprehension about the enormous influence of a few critics on this risky market where half of all plays produced did not earn a profit.

One other method Anderson had for controlling the power of the critics was to withhold from them the usual first-night tickets and keep them from seeing or writing about the play until it had run a few weeks. He did this in connection with the opening of *Joan of Lorraine* and *Anne of the Thousand Days;*[120] and, though both plays had long runs, whether or not any of their success can be attributed to his ticket control is questionable. In 1946 Anderson's quarrel with the drama critics came to a head after they had unanimously belabored *Truckline Cafe,* one of his weakest endeavors. The play's producers advertised in the *New York Times* that the critics were unqualified by either training or taste to judge plays; and Anderson himself then assaulted them in the *New York Herald Tribune* on March 4. Under the heading "To the Theatre Public" he declared that many of the critics were incompetent and irresponsible; moreover, they constituted a kind of "Jukes family" in journalism![121] About two months before *Anne of the Thousand Days* opened in late

1948, Anderson printed in the *Tribune* his "More Thoughts about Dramatic Critics," a calmer but no less bitter summary of his beliefs about the "censorship" that critics imposed, the undoubted tendency of producers to bow to adverse notices, the economic pinch, and the unfairness of not permitting Americans at large to determine what plays would thrive on Broadway and hence throughout the nation.[122] Avery is justified in asserting that Anderson's was a "slight misappropriation of blame," for he cudgeled the critics rather than the general public that accepted so readily whatever the critics said.[123]

Anderson not only assailed the critics but the art of the motion pictures, and he wrote an essay full of damnation on this last subject.[124] As he saw it, the supreme loss for the playwright was for him to die early as a creative dramatist and to end up tinkering on motion picture scripts in Hollywood.[125] Ironically, he spent at least three decades writing the hated scenarios! — for the money. Like many of his contemporary artists, he simply could not resist such a big reward for his labors, especially since commercial returns from Broadway plays (even well-patronized ones) grew so uncertain during the inflationary spiral of the post-World War II years. Such film scripts provided a large portion of his own income.[126] His own plays often went into films: they include *Anne of the Thousand Days, Key Largo, Knickerbocker Holiday, Mary of Scotland, Saturday's Children* ("Maybe it's Love," in 1935, is supposed to be the fifth motion picture version), *Bad Seed, The Eve of St. Mark, Elizabeth the Queen* (entitled "The Private Lives of Elizabeth and Essex"), *What Price Glory* (filmed 1926, 1936, 1952), and *Winterset*. The sale of film rights to these plays must have been particularly lucrative for him: The Playwrights' Producing Company, in whose profits he shared handsomely, sold *The Eve of St. Mark* for three hundred thousand dollars,[127] *Bad Seed* for three hundred thousand dollars, and *Joan of Lorraine* for two hundred and fifty thousand dollars.[128] As additional income, he received ten percent of the gross receipts whenever he had a stage play running,[129] plus sizeable royalties from the sheet music and phonograph recordings of "September Song" taken from *Knickerbocker Holiday*.[130] It is almost amusing to find him writing to his daughter, Hesper, in 1956 — a lean year for him — that he was trying hard to get along on a mere thirty-six thousand dollars annually. On the other hand, as his friend and business partner S. N. Behrman put it, Anderson steadfastly believed that "financial stringency was a stimulus to creative effort," that money "devitalized" the artist; accordingly, he quickly gave away to his family whatever he earned.[131] He was most generous.

CHAPTER 2

War as Destroyer and
Touchstone of Character

TO begin a study of Maxwell Anderson's drama with one of his war plays in verse form is appropriate because the theme of war inheres in his first stage success and because he ultimately achieved his greatest fame with verse drama. The Romantic in him often gravitated to bygone eras and to famous historical figures who were involved in war, in political intrigue, in giving birth to great ideas, or in some combination of these activities. For a man who never saw military experience and who practiced pacifism for many years, it is certainly surprising that he wrote so many war plays; however, like many armchair strategists, he may have envied those charmed souls who enter the smoke and hell of combat and finally emerge alive, bearing a wealth of almost incommunicable experience that is in some ways forever denied the uninitiated because it is so personal and so strange, perhaps so ghastly. Only the earliest of these plays by Anderson can be considered antiwar in a satirical sense, but all the others at least disapprove of war as a destroyer of lives and of values; but, bad as war is, these plays show it to be, paradoxically, a touchstone of character. World War II inspired in Anderson a whole knapsack of plays that were strong in patriotic sentiment but usually weak in enduring qualities. They generally suffer from a lack of esthetic distance and, to a lesser extent, personal military experience.

I Valley Forge

Anderson chose the dramatically correct moment in the past for the beginning of his verse play *Valley Forge* (1934) — the crisis period of January, 1778, a month when supplies were scarce for the Continental Army during the American Revolution, as history tells us. The play itself explains in part that General Washington had recently lost several battles; some officers and politicians were agitating for his removal from command; and he had retreated into the wilds of Pennsylvania to lick his wounds. The winter was a very bitter one; and during the January thaw, commissary wagons loaded with vital supplies were unnecessarily delayed on the way to Valley Forge; meanwhile, the suffering troops complained and waited for a dilatory Congress to send help. Camp fever, smallpox, and hunger ravaged the eleven thousand Continentals, about a fourth of whom were unfit for duty for lack of shoes and clothing (Anderson in his play points up this lack by having a sentry stand guard in his hat so that his toes will not freeze).

Consequently, many of the soldiers deserted rather than freeze or starve to death and be buried in unmarked graves. General Washington felt that only the most extraordinary efforts could keep the tiny army from disbanding. January of 1778 was the critical time in another sense; for, since Martha Washington was not to arrive in camp for another month, the arrival of Washington's love in his youth, Mary Philipse, is that much more possible.[1] The following February would have been a trifle less suitable so far as the soldiers were concerned, because their period of intense suffering would have been almost over; there is some evidence that the hardships eased slightly in the fourth week, although Washington's own letters tell a story of dreadful privation far into the month.[2]

We first meet in the play some of the grumbling soldiers whose fortitude under suffering later inspires General Washington to continue with the war. The arrival of the British General Howe's dog in camp provides the excuse for having one soldier return the animal to the enemy forces in Philadelphia; the dog is thus a small but effective dramatic device for slipping in the next scene, which is a ball in Howe's headquarters whose luxury contrasts with the pitiful privations in the other army. Howe induces the lovely Mrs. Mary Philipse Morris, a lady already eager to renew an old love suit with Washington, to visit the American general and to convince him of the hopelessness of additional combat. (Her name is usually abbreviated to Mary Philipse in the play, doubtless to emphasize her erstwhile maidenly status and her availability as a love partner.) She will also unwittingly convey the lie that the hoped-for, American-French Alliance will not occur. Arriving at Valley Forge disguised in comic opera fashion in man's clothing, she tempts Washington to a love dalliance; but he is devoted to the Revolution, and excuses

himself as being too old for an amour, though the historical
Washington was then a virile forty-five.

In one of the best scenes, General Washington receives two shifty
Congressmen who have been negotiating behind his back with
Howe for peace terms because the prolonged war has diminished
profits from trade; he feeds them some of the standard fare of putrid
camp rations and then throws them bodily out the door — theater
audiences in Washington, D. C. howled at this scene! Before the
visitors leave, they sting him with the news that not all of his generals support either him or the war. This message constitutes the
recognition scene that Anderson had started using early in the
1930's: Washington realizes for the first time that he can count for
support on neither Congress nor all his generals. As a result, he
arranges to parley with Howe; and he is on the verge of surrender
even after he learns that there actually is an American-French Alliance now; but, at the last minute, the heroic example of some of his
soldiers present accidentally at the parley, as well as Mary's love for
him, save him from capitulation.[3]

As is typical of Anderson with his history plays, he did the necessary research[4] and then bent the facts of history to suit his needs.
For example, the whole Mary Philipse incident seems pure invention. Her visit is not impossible since the woman did exist and since
there was no rival spouse at Valley Forge in January, 1778, to dis-
courage her visit; nonetheless, the real Mary would have been
middle-aged by then and lacking in siren appeal. Anderson also
wisely omits to mention her husband who was then a prisoner of the
Continental Army and thus obviates some otherwise distracting
material such as inquiries about his health and safety. No doubt he
introduced Mary into the play to show something of the human side
of Washington, a figure ordinarily difficult to portray with sufficient
realism on the stage because of his godlike stature in the popular
mind. We are led to believe that, if Washington can resist Mary's
seductiveness, he might conceivably have the strength to resist the
temptation of surrender on the field of war. Moreover, Mary
Philipse is a useful dramatic link between the two armies. Since the
historic Mrs. Loring in Philadelphia, another married woman who
also figures in the play, indirectly helped by her charms to keep
Howe off the battlefield, her role may have suggested to Anderson
the use of a counterpart figure with which to tempt Washington.

According to history, Howe actually sent the terms of surrender to General Washington, whereas in the play he presents them during a face-to-face conference while Mary is present. The two commanders never met during the war, but the fictional meeting is powerfully effective in underscoring the crisis in faith that Washington was suffering. News of the American-French Alliance first reached General Washington on May 6, 1778, rather than in the preceding January. As for the justification for all such juggling of facts, Anderson availed himself of the age-old license of the storyteller.

Valley Forge has a nobility and a timeless relevance for Americans in war or in peace who hesitate in loyalty or who backslide from patriotism. To support the exalted theme of a noble man's conquest over despair, the language assigned to Washington and to certain of his officers has dignity and polish; at times, the diction has even a restrained beauty, as where Lafayette moves our hearts by actually apologizing for his effusive, albeit sincere, utterance. Lafayette shares the author's distrust of rhetoric; yet, like him, he seems to know that the impassioned moment demands a suitably elevated language. On the other hand, Washington's own language, for example, is sometimes quite vivid and realistic — though he does have some purple speech near the end — which partakes of the *flavor* of the military camp as well as of the profanity to which the actual figure was sometimes prone. Mabel D. Bailey is mistaken in claiming it improbable that this general would dare tell some of his brave and ragged soldiers that most men are fools (Act I, Scene i); what she has done is wrench the passage from its context.[5] In the long speech in which the passage occurs, Washington is talking about the capacity of people everywhere to govern themselves wisely; and the only specific fools he cites — the real objects of his ire — are those in the Continental Congress; and for them he intended no personal insult. Moreover, his words are directed toward some soldiers who have threatened to desert the army, a grave offense to any officer and one sufficient to provoke the frankest response, even though Washington's response is mild and reasonable.

I also disagree with John H. Lawson's contention that Washington is "so devitalized and over-simplified that something outside his real interests must be introduced to humanize him."[6] By both speech

and action, this Washington is a sturdy, manly figure who is terrible
in anger, compassionate toward his men, and capable of suffering —
as great men sometimes are — from the ingratitude of others, such
as members of the Continental Congress. His character had to be
simplified *somewhat* to fit into the limited war situation in which
Anderson chose to show him; but, within this situation, he is entirely plausible. It is simply too much to demand that the whole
multi-faceted man be there: planter, horticulturist, fox hunter, inde-
fatigable dancer, justice of the peace, cattle breeder, politician,
gambler, etc. And, although Mary Philipse was not one of his "real
interests" at the time, she does, as said before, contribute much to
the unity of the play and in no way seems out of place in an era in
which women at times did inhabit camps of war. As a matter of
historical record, there were several women of good standing at
Valley Forge starting in February, 1778. The historical Washington
offers formidable problems, however, to any dramatist wanting to
portray him seriously; for there is hardly a weakness with which to
make him seem human in these days of the search for the anti-hero;
nor can he be the subject of tragedy since there is neither tragic flaw
nor final defeat. In short, there is little or nothing to detract from
the monumental greatness in him that Americans and Europeans
alike have insisted upon honoring.

Gerald Rabkin objects with some fairness that Maxwell Anderson
in planning this drama was unfortunately "tied to the facts of history" because, in making Washington triumph, he was espousing
the powerful, rebellious, antigovernmental hero who could conceivably fit the dictatorial type that Anderson elsewhere loathes.[7] The
answer is that Washington, within the action of the play, poses no
hazards for democracy; for he is not yet, at least, a leader in government and an abuser of power. As Washington is portrayed in this
work, he has a bitter insight into the weaknesses of men of power
that would presumably have been a healthful preventive.

In the first stage performance, the role of Washington went to the
English actor Philip Merivale after he reportedly thrice refused the
part.[8] *Valley Forge* opened in Pittsburgh on November 19, 1934 and
the next month went to New York City where it had a mere fifty-
eight performances — a commercial failure. The reviews were
mixed. Brooks Atkinson in the *New York Times* spoke for many of
the reviewers in confessing that this play was not one of Anderson's
better ones but that it had merits in the magnificent portrayal of

Washington, in the well-motivated scenes, and in the elevated subject matter. Edith J. R. Isaacs in *Theatre Arts Monthly* found fault with both the writing and the production. In *The Nation*, the scholarly Joseph W. Krutch thought the play romantically entertaining but the language almost too literary. Most of the later commentators in books about American drama have somehow not been moved by *Valley Forge*, although William E. Taylor goes so far as to assert that it is Anderson's noblest play.[9] The work suffers undeservedly from critical neglect.

Some of *Valley Forge*'s failure on the stage could have been due to unfortunate timing: America in 1934 was between wars; moreover, it was gripped by an economic depression for which our people felt little cause to be grateful to the Founding Fathers who had set in motion the machinery of such a fallible and helpless Republic. The winter of Anderson's brooding discontent with Congress, which had raged unchecked through *Both Your Houses*, swept also into *Valley Forge* and is expressed in General Sterling's acid remarks about Congress. The public had not yet good cause to praise the incoming New Deal wonder workers under Franklin D. Roosevelt, many of whose measures to regenerate the economy Anderson approved of.[10] On the other hand, in the context of the times, and they were desperate ones, the play must also be seen as a call to faith in the national purpose despite the shortcomings of government; that, though hunger and unemployment haunt the nation, the situation was much worse at *Valley Forge* — in the "depression" phase of the Revolutionary War — and yet Washington had overcome *his* doubts and had fought on to ultimate victory.

II   What Price Glory

What Price Glory started in the editorial rooms of the *World* when Laurence Stallings reminisced to Anderson about his combat experiences in the American Expeditionary Force in France, during which he had suffered in the fierce battle at Belleau Wood a wound so severe that a leg had had to be amputated.[11] One hero figuring in these anecdotes was Philip Townsend Case, the captain of the Fifth Marine Regiment in which Stallings had been a lieutenant. "Stallings used to say," a friend of his commented, "that Case was the most extraordinary commanding officer he had ever seen — if Case had been in charge of the Army he would have fought right on to

Berlin." In the subsequent portrayal of Captain Flagg, the facts apply to Case; but the swaggering features of Flagg were derived from another captain known to Stallings.[12]

Working at night, Anderson used Stallings' notes to write a draft of four acts, the first two of these acts conforming closely in plot to the material of Act I in the published play, and the last two acts to Acts II and III, respectively.[13] Various sources indicate that Act II, as we know it today, was originally weak in local color — specifically, it lacked the racy, salty vernacular indigenous to front-line marines — and Stallings made appropriate changes in it. Some commentators claim that Stallings wrote the entire second act[14] — which *is* stylistically different from the other two — but the best available evidence shows that he only re-worked what Anderson had already written.[15] Stallings also found a producer, Arthur Hopkins, for *What Price Glory*, which soon became the winner of the season.[16] As soon as success was assured, Anderson resigned from the *World;* and, feeling like celebrating yet not knowing what to do, he bought a cane and strolled up and down Fifth Avenue, flourishing it before curious passers-by; meanwhile, Stallings bought himself a Hispano-Swiza.[17] One of Anderson's happiest days must have been when his former drama professor, Koch, visited him in New York after the play had become a hit, and he was able to tell his dear "Proff" (as the students liked to spell it) that he was receiving a thousand dollars a week in royalties.[18]

The setting of *What Price Glory* is France during World War I, and the profane and tough professional marine Captain Flagg competes with his long-time rival Sergeant Quirt for the affections of a slut named Charmaine. Quirt narrowly escapes being forced to marry the girl when her father protests to Flagg, the commanding officer, that Quirt had deflowered his *petite enfante innocente*. Act II, set in a wine cellar of a French town, is wrought in the spirit of bloody Naturalism that brings out effectively the misery and bitterness and havoc of war. Dirty marines talk about the fighting and the casualties as various wounded are brought in; a callous pharmacist mate prepares for surgical operations; a lieutenant, hysterical from combat fatigue, breaks down at seeing an injured fellow officer. In this portion of the drama, the crusty Flagg reveals at last his basically tender nature when he comforts the hysterical lieutenant. Act III re-unites the quarreling pair of marines in the tavern of Charmaine's father, and they decide to let a game of cards determine which one will win the girl. Again, a call to arms interrupts the dispute; at first, Flagg resists going, but the professional in him rallies; and Quirt cannot resist the clarion call to duty any more than Flagg can.[19]

Despite the vigorous, hairy-chested realism of this play, there is really little exploration of character; most of the characterization may be found in connection with Captain Flagg in Act II. Charmaine is, of course, never anything but an insignificant flirt — she is not even close to being an endangered civilian. In fact, a measure of truth exists in Jordan Miller's protest that the characters "lack the emotional depth so badly needed to display the havoc that warfare creates within a man's soul. . . ."[20] But that *What Price Glory* is as much a diverting comedy as it is a serious antiwar play helps to explain this shortcoming, for had the authors wanted to make a concerted effort to uncover the hideous face of war, they would have introduced, for instance, civilian casualties and destruction of property; or they might have used as heroes some draftees upon whose unhardened sensibilities the horrors of combat could be shown to greater advantage (as Erich Maria Remarque did in *All Quiet on the Western Front*). Although Flagg and Quirt elect to continue the holocaust without seriously questioning its means or its ends, the play gives the final impression that war is hell, but what can or will anyone do to change that?

Nevertheless, Anderson and Stallings adversely criticize military glory and thereby gratified a postwar audience who had become disillusioned about the "war to end all wars." The terribly serious second act is crowded between two funny ones, yet we are always aware that real danger and death lurk in the wings in the form of some sudden, pointless military engagement that is ready to engulf the heroes and to end forever all laughter. And, because the object of the heroes' quarrel is a mere trifle of a slut, we are ready to believe that the object of the whole bloody war itself is no less inglorious and foolish.

What Price Glory rang up around four hundred performances during its long Broadway engagement and its tours, and the drama critics were in general friendly to the play. Burns Mantle reported that *What Price Glory* was "unquestionably the dramatic success of the [1924–25] season."[21] Barrett H. Clark opined that for "the first time in any play we were shown the doughboy as he really was — rough-mannered, loose-tongued, cynical, and gullible — not in the least as he had been portrayed by sentimental writers of musical comedies."[22]

Despite Clark's praise, the supposed linguistic indecencies provoked an uproar at the time. Various public officials, including the mayor of New York City and some high military officers of the Navy and Marine Corps, were irritated by the language uttered by the stage marines. City police objected to the profanity, and even the United States District Attorney investigated the play for possible violation of Federal law in discrediting the Marine Corps. But no legal suit was brought against the play, probably because Arthur Hopkins voluntarily cut out from the script some twenty words that had offended the police.[23] Amid this furor a Unitarian preacher, Reverend Charles F. Potter, bravely came to the defense of the original play: "wonderful portrayal of the brutality of the professional soldier. . . ."[24] Indeed, *What Price Glory's* unconventional psychology and earthy language, though thought shocking at the time, prepared the way for a more intense realism in the theater.

III   Key Largo

Anderson's little-known and hitherto unpublished "The Bastion Saint-Gervais," broadcast as a radio play in late May, 1938, is evidently an early attempt to formulate the ideological crisis of the battlefield that entered the Prologue of *Key Largo*. In "Gervais," four young Americans defend a hopeless fortification in Spain against the advancing armies of Franco; as the remnant of a company of volunteers, they now hold the line after the other troops have pulled back; and, although they are bitter, they will not quit and run. This fifteen-page playlet is informed with much the same passion for democracy as well as the same persistent doubts about statecraft that we find in *Key Largo*; but, unlike the characters in *Key Largo*, all the young men of *Gervais* choose to fight after they have aired their points of view. As the curtain goes down, they blaze away at hundreds of enemy soldiers climbing the hill toward them. Because of this idealistic stance, the action of the drama can go no further since all the heroes will be dead in no time at all.

Gervais, as well as *Key Largo*, represent Anderson's role as the prophet of World War II — and he is one who is calling here for resistance against the new fascism in Europe. There is still another influence on the making of *Key Largo*: Maxwell Anderson wrote in a letter to Kate Klugston that the title of *Key Largo*, as well as the plot, were due to an occurrence, not otherwise described, that happened during the winter of 1938–39 when he was motoring through Key Largo, Florida.[25] Whatever the origins, *Key Largo* is clearly superior to his earlier war play *What Price Glory* because it is better at probing soldiers' responsibilities to each other and to themselves.[26] The new drama appeared on the stage in late 1939 and ran for one hundred and five performances.

The Prologue of *Key Largo*, which is essential to an understanding of later developments, shows the young American King McCloud, who had led a group of idealistic men to fight on the Loyalist side of the Spanish Civil War, pull out of battle after he had tried in vain to convince his companions to do likewise because the war was lost. Worse still for his conscience, which begins to trouble him, he gets captured by the enemy and agrees to fight for them in return for sparing his life. One of the doomed companions who elects to stay behind is Victor d'Alcala, whose sister Alegre, back in Key Largo, has secretly fallen in love with McCloud. After the war, McCloud feels a compulsion to visit each of the families of his slain companions, to report how they came to die, and to seek penance for his tortured soul; but each time he makes such a visit he feels despised.

Meanwhile, in Key Largo, the gangster Murillo and his cronies, protected by the local sheriff, have taken by force a cabin in the tourist camp of Victor's blind father and Alegre. When McCloud arrives at this place, he tells his tale to the girl, remembering that Victor had said she was the one person in all the world who would be sure to give understanding and forgiveness for a crime committed. Victor's father and sister dislike McCloud's turncoat act, but they make him feel wanted by asking him to stay and defend them from the hoodlums. McCloud realizes that he will now have a chance to atone for the old disgrace, yet he also knows that, if faced with dying for a so-called worthy cause, he will not be able to trust his "treacherous, casuistic brain" that will sieze upon any handy reason for staying alive. And, when Murillo confronts him with a gun, McCloud shrinks again and surrenders.

The second and final act of the play provides his last chance to redeem himself. The night before McCloud's arrival, Murillo had murdered a road-gang foreman and had sunk his body in the Gulf of Mexico. D'Alcala persuades two fugitive but innocent Indians —

symbolic of another lost cause, the struggle of the redskin against the white man — to raise the body and to let it float ashore so that the sheriff will be compelled to take action against the gangster leader. The sheriff, however, who needs someone to arrest and to whom justice is irrelevant, accuses the Indians; and, if Alegre will not inform him about their whereabouts, McCloud will have to bear the indictment since he has already pretended to be d'Alcala's son against whom the sheriff has an old charge. Hence, the turncoat has unwittingly trapped himself even in his innocence; like other tragic heroes, he has cut away his own underpinnings. To protect McCloud, Alegre steers the sheriff to the Indians' hiding place, believing that once the Indians have been brought back and McCloud has to confront them, he will nobly choose their liberty over his own. And this is the choice he makes.

At this juncture, when King McCloud's pessimism comes to a head and causes him to examine in ruthless detail what he considers to be the eggshell basis of the kind of faith d'Alcala and Alegre have, Anderson's poetry soars to heights reached by few other Americans. The poetry is by no means equal to Shakespeare's, of course, but it is effective as an integral part of the dramatic situation. After d'Alcala speaks some powerful Existentialist lines in support of faith in a godless universe, McCloud asks him where the human race is steering; and to this the blind man replies, using the metaphor of space exploration, "To a conquest of all there is, whatever there is / among the suns and stars."[27] When McCloud then asks, what if the universe is empty of any supernaturalism and significance, his question echoes Epicurus' view of the gods as indifferent to man's needs and interests. More especially, his question has a modern tone with its spirit of negation and alienation and emptiness; it brings up a complex of factors in modern civilization such as technology, political institutions deaf to human needs, the breakdown of traditional religious order and certainty caused partly by the new sciences and their gospel of materialism and skepticism, partly by the insights afforded us by various thinkers such as Sigmund Freud, Friedrich Nietzsche, Karl Marx, and Soren Kierkegaard.

But the playwright's persona, d'Alcala, has the answer for McCloud, which is Anderson's cosmic philosophy. The substance of the answer is that again and again man rises from the mud of the evolutionary processes; looks about; realizes, to his immense distress, that he is alone on a godless planet; and then sinks back frightened. Repeatedly, he makes a religion out of his hope, follows it to the uttermost limits, and then the sense of aloneness strikes him like a blight. In spite of this recurrent disappointment, however, man has a high destiny: he will someday be able to "face even the stars without despair. . . ."[28] In this way, d'Alcala renders not only a brilliant poetic explanation of the sickness of our times, the mind's subtle attack on itself, but also his hope that man must and will persevere in a godless universe and be guided, perhaps, by some high purpose as vague yet sure as the faint star-glimmer of hope that Edward A. Robinson holds out for us.

Anderson's cosmic philosophy, which makes no provision for a soul or for an afterlife, probably satisfies some agnostics and atheists; indeed, much of his appeal as a thinker may lie in precisely this adjustment to the religious atrophy and yet continued spiritual yearning of the modern world. Nonetheless, what we find in his philosophy is, for many of us, a not particularly consoling *Verzweifelungsmüt* (courage of despair). After the removal of the Christian feast, there remains only poor man's porridge. But such courage is welcome, and it is far from being shallow. And this affirmation of courage in the play is all the more effective because it comes from a *blind* man, one who had lost his sight while fighting for an earlier worthwhile cause in Spain.

Near the end of the play, McCloud, ennobled by the love of the girl and perhaps by her father's eloquent idealism, finally makes up his mind and takes a stand against Murillo and his gang. But by then, unfortunately, he has already set in motion those forces which will destroy him. Incidentally, the fact that this hero does take a stand, though he forfeits his life in the process, is an implicit rejoinder to some of Anderson's critics who hold that the playwright is a defeatist who always takes the easy way out of the great problems that he raises.

Key Largo, though hewing to Anderson's announced guide for tragedy, is surely by any of his own requirements a lesser achievement, despite some lovely passages and the final nobility of the hero. The play lacks, somehow, the feeling for heroic grandeur inherent in the acknowledged high tragedies of Aeschylus, Sophocles, Euripides, and Marlowe. Probably Maxwell Anderson would have been the first to admit that McCloud is simply not in the same exalted company with Prometheus and Othello who, through their sufferings, fill us with awe and terror that somehow illuminate both the heights and depths of human responsiveness. Sometimes we can also measure a play by the stature of lesser characters, such as the villains; but, in *Key Largo*, such characters are close to being stereotypes of the big city hoodlum and crooked provincial lawman. Another failing of the play is that the poetry is not of a consistently high level throughout.

We have to conclude that the application of Anderson's rules was not in itself sufficient to guarantee him a high tragedy, any more than did the *Poetics* serve Pierre Corneille in his tragedies based on ancient themes. While I admit that the dramatic hero today may come from the common walks of life, as McCloud does, I would yet rank this play below Arthur Miller's *Death of a Salesman*, which is still a model for the poetized (non-verse) treatment of a similarly universal theme that has tragic implications.

IV   Candle in the Wind *and* The Eve of St. Mark

The period of World War II during which *Candle in the Wind* first reached the public — namely, September, 1941 — was a dark one indeed for the Allies because Poland, Denmark, Norway, the Low Countries, and France had already fallen to the German hordes; Britain was under aerial bombardment; and even vast Russia seemed on the verge of defeat. Anderson's play reflects the desperation of the times. The story, a weak one nonetheless, concerns a celebrated American actress, Madeline Guest, who is in Paris just after the German invasion of France and who plots to release her French lover, Raoul St. Cloud, from the clutches of the Nazi oppressors. Thanks to her, he is at last free and on his way to England; but she is now trapped in France.

There is simply not much to praise in this dramatic effusion of patriotic sentiment. Only the external considerations of the production — the story's timeliness, Helen Hayes in the lead role, Anderson's reputation, and the dearth of good plays on Broadway during the war years — could account for the play's remarkable run of ninety-five performances. Far better Anderson plays have had shorter runs. I agree with Avery that one cause for *Candle*'s artistic failure is that Anderson, deeply troubled about the Nazi threat to the free world, did not employ in his art the necessary esthetic distance.[29] On the other hand, Anderson clearly required personal experience when he was writing about the wars of his own day: it will be remembered that it was Stallings who had contributed the decisive element of the battlefield in *Glory*. Anderson worked best when the Romantic in him, enamored of historical backgrounds, chose for his era a remote time when not only the esthetic distance was more manageable but when the demands of realism, in the form of personal experience, would not be overly pressing.

A better coverage of the war came the next year in *The Eve of St. Mark*, perhaps the only Anderson play based rather closely upon the people and the places he actually knew. After touring the "provinces," the work opened at the Cort Theatre on October 7, 1942 and ran for all of three hundred and seven performances. Anderson chose not to attend that premiere; but, when he later asked a friend how it went, " 'Marvelously,' the friend answered. 'The audience wouldn't leave the theater. They just sat there and applauded. There could have been 10 more curtain calls.' "[30] In respect to mere popularity, this third war play bears comparison with *Glory;* on the other hand, in its attitude toward war, it is altogether different. By this time in his life, Anderson was passionately and actively caught up in the fight for freedom, had already lost a nephew in the war, and had seen two of this three sons enter the military services. Incidentally, he donated a large percentage of the profits from this play to agencies engaged in war relief.

In this play, Quizz West, a virtuous but passionate farm boy in the army, meets in New York the girl Janet from his own district, falls in love with her, and presents her to his family when he goes on leave again. Thereafter, throughout the play, tender domestic scenes alternate with amusing military ones. Before Quizz and Janet have a chance to consummate their love or to marry, he is sent to an obscure island in the Philipines to fight the Japanese invaders. The defense is brave but hopeless. In the legend associated with the Eve of St. Mark (note the Keatsian echo), a virgin at the church door will have a vision of all those parishioners who will die that year; and, if her lover is among them, he will turn and gaze at her, perhaps speak.

Accordingly, in the second half of the drama, where the battle action occurs, there are two dream sections (Act II) in which Quizz knowingly communicates by spirit with his sleeping mother and then with his girlfriend. He asks their help in solving a problem: whether he should elect to stay to defend the island in a voluntary rear-guard action or to escape by boat to safety. He learns from his extrasensory perception experience that, since his loved ones naturally do not want him to sacrifice himself but to return to them, he himself must bear the burden of deciding. He and his comrades elect to stay — a testimony to the selfless courage of American fighting men — and they know full well that their heroism will cost them their lives. Quizz's decision to stay and die for a cause, rather than back away as McCloud does early in *Key Largo*, is emblematic of the author's new affirmative spirit in behalf of democracy. Some months pass in the story; back at the farm, Quizz's loved ones adjust in their separate ways to the terrible news that the Japanese have captured the island.[31]

For background material for *The Eve of St. Mark*, Anderson visited Fort Bragg, North Carolina, in the spring of 1942. On a company street inside the camp, he chanced to meet a group of raucous soldiers who were good-naturedly confiscating the monthly pay of one of their comrades, a tall, attractive Southerner who was indebted to them. This amusing incident Anderson tells about in his Foreword to Marion Hargrove's *See Here, Private Hargrove*.[32] Among these troopers was Marion Hargrove, a North Carolinian with the golden tongue of an orator, who had continued to contribute a column to the Charlotte, North Carolina *News* even after induction; among his writings for the column were the materials of the forenamed book which Anderson "discovered" in the camp and soon recommended to a publisher, after which the hilarious *See Here, Private Hargrove* became an immediate best seller.

Also in the group of soldiers were a "large dark Irishman" named Thomas James Mulvehill; Lloyd Shearer, possessed of a knack for comic writing; John Bushemi, a photographer for the army newspaper *Yank* (later killed by a Japanese mortar shell at the height of the battle for the island of Eniwetok); and a man named Sher. Later, while drinking beer with Anderson in the Rainbow Grill in nearby Fayetteville, the soldiers wondered whether they should defy military regulations and take him, a civilian, into their barrack to spend the night. Hargrove decided the issue: " 'What the hell? Anderson has won the Pulitzer Prize. Maybe he'll buy us more beer tomorrow.' " The next morning, at reveille, a sergeant kicked the sleeping Anderson in the thigh as he lay there on an army cot, mistaking him for Bushemi, and yelled " 'Outta bed, Bushemi!' " Anderson "awoke with the cry of a wounded bull," according to Shearer; and, told that he had unlawfully trespassed on government property, he wisely fled to his hotel in Fayetteville. By such means the famous Anderson was collecting his local color.

That evening, while dining in the Rainbow Grill that was to become the model for the play's restaurant, Anderson jokingly told Hargrove, Bushemi, and Shearer that he was going to put them into a play — " 'Maybe as grave diggers.' " Six months later — though it took Anderson only about two months to do the play[33] — the trio of enlisted men journeyed to New York City and checked on a report that their unusual visitor had a play in rehearsal. As Shearer told it later, he was pleasantly struck by the similarities in the names (Francis Marion, Buscemi, Shevlin, Thomas Mulveroy); their jokes that Anderson had adapted; the army barrack; and the grill. (The play's cast was astonished to learn that here were the originals they were portraying!) On the other hand, Shearer admitted that Anderson had taken some "liberties" by, for example, having Corporal Hargrove, who had but once *seen* an artillery gun, be a crack marksman with that weapon, and also by having him uncannily able to resist a "blond bit of fleshy temptation."[34]

As for the farm scenes in *The Eve of St. Mark*, Avery notes that most of the people there are patterned after the families of Dan and Lela Chambers; for Lela's mail to her famous brother reveals sundry anecdotes and occurrences that he employed in dramatizing farm life.[35] Alan Anderson informed me in his letter of May 5, 1973, that his father got other farm details from the family of Ralph and Ethel Chambers (another of the sisters). Additionally, Maxwell Anderson had the farm experiences of his own youth to draw upon. Alan, while stationed at Fort Dix, New Jersey, had sent his father letters containing descriptions of army training procedures as well as comic dialogues about the training. Lela's son Sergeant Lee Chambers, a pilot downed and lost in the Mediterranean area early in the war, seems to have been the prototype for Quizz West; and the play is appropriately dedicated to Chambers' memory.

On the basis of what Anderson evidently confided to Robert Rice, he pursued in *The Eve of St. Mark* a method of construction "fairly typical" of him by beginning with the recognition scene involving the protagonist and by then looking for supporting characters. As mentioned earlier, his method of finding those characters for the present story was *un*typical; also untypical was the integration of two poetic dream sections (Act II, Scenes iv and v) — the latter of which contains the recognition scene — in an otherwise prose medium,

for the poetry represented to the dramatist the emotional climax of
the drama and was needed to convey an exaltation that prose cannot
furnish. Anderson added, "Certainly there's no play without it." It
depressed him, however, that this was the very passage that people
supposedly disliked[36] — though he was surely hypersensitive on
this alleged criticism. The poetry itself, as a matter of fact, caused
hardly a ripple of discontent; such poetry of his sometimes passed on
the stage for fine prose. The difficulty must have been that the
dream scenes, so unrealistic — nay so improbable in their use of
spiritual communication — arrived after the audience had already
enjoyed some of the most hilarious and colorfully realistic material
about the stateside army camp and its environs that Anderson had
yet produced for the stage. Act I, Scene iv, which is laid in the
Moonbow Restaurant, is notably rich in piquant, genuine vernacular such as we would expect to hear on the lips of soldiers and their
women. Each of the characters is credibly drawn and suitably differentiated; and, though the subjects of conversation in the restaurant are trivial and are typical of army life they are nonetheless
interestingly conceived. Especially well done is the part where two
pretty girls enter, summon Mulveroy aside, and talk with him about
arranging a double date. When tipsy Lill, one of the two over-
dressed girls of easy virtue at the table with Marion and Quizz,
observes them, she hears from Marion the absurd explanation —
which she believes! — that Mulveroy is the girls' spiritual mentor
and gives them religious tutelage. In their order of diminishing
effectiveness, the restaurant and barrack scenes are at the very top;
they are followed next by the farm scenes; but those laid in the
Pacific, which were those most remote from Anderson's private
experience, are last.[37]

The dream passages are not the only troublesome parts of *The Eve
of St. Mark*. Professor Lee Norvelle, a friend of Anderson's and the
director of the first amateur production, was sure that the hero was
not Quizz West, contrary to what the author had intended, but
Francis Marion; and he directed the play accordingly. Though Anderson was not unpleased with Norvelle's version, he never agreed
with him about the hero status of Marion; he did concede, however,
that many other people felt as Norvelle did.[38] Marion is at least
equally interesting as West, and even more so with regard to his
vivid, comic dialogue. He wins our approval for expressing the kind

of heroism that is adapted for, or at least fashionable with, the intellectual of our times — the man who is hard-boiled, cynical, and wary about the oftentimes needless wars for worthless real estate, but who is brave enough in time of crisis to gaze straight down the barrel of danger without flinching if he knows the battle is a just one.

Late in Act II, Marion drops his habitual ornate jauntiness and soberly asks whether his comrades and he are certain it is worthwhile to die in order to save the free world. Of course he has already made up his mind in the affirmative: his is merely a harmless rhetorical question voiced to show that he is, unlike the enemy, no mere cannon fodder stumbling blindly to his death. Marion here wears a tough-minded front to cover his patriot soul. Private West, by comparison, is the gentle man of obvious sentiment whose heart is always on his sleeve. We witness his feeding of the neglected sheep, his sterling devotion to his sweetheart Janet despite the easy availability of the restaurant girls, and his heart-wringing address to Janet in the second dream scene. He is best in Act I, Scene v, when he and Janet, impassioned from long separation and urgent yearning, want to consummate their love but realize that they need a house of their own; in fact, they disclose a beautiful, tender inexperience that is so genuine as to be almost embarrassing.

The play's ending is, however, patriotically overdone if it is measured by the tastes of today; for, inspired by Quizz's sacrifice to make the world better, his brothers announce that they are about to enter the armed forces to carry on their share of the burden. "Very moving," even "profoundly moving," ran two contemporary reviews. But most later commentators, especially those of the postwar years, label *The Eve of St. Mark* as sentimental and as Romantically superficial. Characteristic of this new taste is Bailey who finds fault with the "unalleviated purity of sentiment and conduct";[39] these are features, nevertheless, which will help make this play most difficult to revive in our era of increased cynicism and sexual experience, and of the popular depiction of the anti-hero. The play is a product of and almost exclusively for its own era, for hardly anyone not alive at the time of the American military losses in the Pacific — *The Eve of St. Mark* reached the stage just ten months after the bombing of Pearl Harbor had shocked America to its roots — can appreciate the idealistic fervor of Americans for patriotism and self-sacrifice that went far to make this play a rousing popular success.

V   Storm Operation

During Anderson's visit to North Africa in May and June, 1943 —
a visit arranged by the United States War Department with the
condition that he submit his resulting script for approval — he came
to know the troops and the women attached to the battlefront, along
with the problems many of them shared with respect to the de-
teriorated moral values caused by the war. What Anderson seemingly wanted to accomplish in *Storm Operation* — the title of which
General Dwight Eisenhower supposedly suggested to him during
their interview in Algiers[40] — was mainly some entertaining, high-
class propaganda that would be useful in building troop moral and in
helping bridge an understanding between the battlefield and the
home front.[41] The particular military campaign that Anderson tried
to illuminate was "Torch," the code name for the Allied amphibious
and aerial landings in North Africa that began in the fall of 1942 and
during which about one hundred thousand American and British
troops, most of whom were as yet untested in combat, battled the
vaunted Afrika Korps. This huge invasion led to the Allies' first great
victory in the West.

A bare outline of the plot of *Storm Operation* cannot do justice to
the complexity and variety of the problems that Anderson tackled in
trying to convey to his audience a realistic account of the delicate,
multi-national relationships among the Allied troops and their
women in North Africa. In this curious failure of a play, the American Sergeant Peter Moldau and the Australian nurse Thomasina
(Tommy) Grey, who had courted each other elsewhere, meet in a
tent in embattled Tunisia; and, amid the bustle of setting up military
facilities and equipment, they renew their romance. Part of the
human conflict here is the presence in camp of her latest lover,
Captain Sutton, a married Englishman; another cause of conflict is
that she no longer believes in the values of constancy and marriage
during wartime, while Sergeant Moldau wants to marry her.

In the background of this love triangle — superficially reminiscent of the sergeant-captain tiff in *Glory* — are the amusing technical and public relation feats of Sergeant Simeon, who has bought
himself an Arab girl. Nurse Grey finally decides to cease going with
Captain Sutton (suppressed parts of the original script have her
living with him) and to marry her true love, Moldau. In a late scene,

as German planes strafe the camp and all but the three principals have the sense to find cover, plucky Captain Sutton, who in his youth had studied for the ministry, swallows his jealousy and performs a marriage service for Moldau and Grey with his handy *Book of Common Prayer*.[42]

In setting out to dramatize the theme of the destruction by war of personal values — as exemplified by Miss Grey — Maxwell Anderson sorely handicapped himself from the beginning by agreeing to submit his script to the War Department for approval; for that agency subsequently required him to make certain politic changes among which were his depiction of Miss Grey's sexual looseness and her relationship with the English captain. Robert E. Sherwood, who as advisor to President Roosevelt had read the manuscript, wrote to Anderson reinforcing the government's censorship: in effect, Anderson was to make the nurse an honest woman, because, otherwise, wartime audiences with their emotional involvements would not be able to view the whole play objectively. Neither the War Department nor Sherwood wanted to offend the Australian and British authorities; therefore, in order to get his work staged, Anderson compromised, with the result that he destroyed Grey's credibility — if she ever had any — and also deleted "the more forceful and characterizing language of the soldiers and the less flattering depictions of North Africans. . . ."[43] In general, he made script changes that showed Allied people as properly *admirable* so that audiences could approve. But, ironically, audiences did not approve; they especially objected to the unbelievable characterization of Nurse Grey. This thoroughly propagandized and emasculated melodrama closed after less than three weeks in New York City.

During Anderson's visits to military installations during World War II, he was surprised to discover that the soldiers had sex on their minds so much of the time.[44] This new knowledge of his found its way into *Storm Operation* in subtle ways, despite the censorship; and it helps provide what is in some respects a more intense realism than is found in his earlier war plays. *Storm Operation* fairly bubbles throughout with authentic facts and details of overseas soldier life. But today's reader of the script — a stage revival is almost unthinkable — is almost certain to be struck with something even more impressive: a sense of immense wasted talent expended for the wrong purposes to suit the wrong critics.

VI   Truckline Cafe

Truckline Cafe, written in late 1945,[45] and produced the following February, echoes "White Desert" in its treatment of a man who kills his wife for unfaithfulness. The theme intrigued Anderson not a little because he again used it in the unpublished short story "West Coast, Night" that he wrote in 1947.[46] The time in *Truckline Cafe* is post-World War II; the setting, the California coast. Once again, as in *Storm Operation*, he probes the moral decay that war brings about in the lives of servicemen and their women; moreover, like that other play, this one is by no means vintage Anderson. The work was apparently published in 1946 and then immediately withdrawn because of the bad reception given to the enactment on stage.[47]

In the play, ex-serviceman Mort, who had cohabited with a Polish girl during his escape from a Nazi prison, returns to California and finds his wife Anne working in a highway cafe. Anne had long before given up her husband for dead and had lived for a while with another man; when she sees Mort again, she tries to conceal her infidelity. In the subplot, also on the subject of sexual transgression, a wife named Tory tries to keep her husband from learning that she had had trysts with his buddy — in nearby cabin #5, no less. Her husband, Sage, suspects the truth; he recognizes the cabin as the one his friend had unwittingly described as using with a woman; then he shoots Tory. Mort, repentant about his adultery and still loving Anne, brings his illegitimate child into the cafe in a patently sentimental effort to win her back (the mother of the child had been shot by the Germans). But Anne rejects them both. Then Sage, who returns in remorse from the murder of his wife, causes Anne to realize that she, too, has made a dreadful mistake in condemning and rejecting her loved one; whereupon, she and Mort accept each other's past and are soon amorously reconciled. If there is any lesson in *Truckline Cafe*, it is to affirm the value of such enduring things as true love, the marriage vow, and the forgiveness of sins.

Almost all the serious critics panned *Truckline Cafe*, which survived for only thirteen performances. Burton Roscoe in the *World-Telegram* moaned, "Anderson . . . Writes an Agony Column"; John Chapman in the *Daily News* armed the title of his review with such barbs as "Hits His Low" and "Dreadful." As a result, Anderson and the producers, as we mentioned earlier, shot back with their own futile animadversions about the supposed bad taste and irresponsible power of the critics. But the play *is* a thin, uninspired, tabloid kind of entertainment, of a level commonly seen in made-for-television scripts nowadays. Not only is the melodrama unacceptable as art, but the main and subplots parallel each other too obviously, too coincidentally, to be acceptable. Moreover, the subplot is not sufficiently subordinated to the main one, with the result that in the Broadway production the actor Marlon Brando, who took the role of Sage, "stole the show."[48] The problem was therefore partly one of mis-casting, and maybe bad stage direction; but I cannot help feeling that, as the script now stands, any competent actor — and Brando just happened to be an outstanding one — would make Sage the center of attention simply because he is the most outwardly exciting and excitable figure in the play. Mort wins only our grudging sympathy; he never engages our deeper feelings. Future generations, of course, will judge Maxwell Anderson by other and far better creations than *Truckline Cafe*.

Sad and strange it is that, of all the war plays the immensely talented Anderson worked on, only the untypical *What Price Glory*, co-written with a tenth-rate author, is commonly printed in anthologies today. Better choices are *Valley Forge* and *Key Largo*, though neither is a masterpiece. Anderson stopped writing war plays in 1945; thereafter, the "cold war" between America and Soviet Russia absorbed his attention, as exemplified in the text and preface of *Barefoot in Athens*.

CHAPTER 3

Of Sceptred and Elected Races

FLAMING forth sporadically in the war plays, the genius of Maxwell Anderson burns more steadily in the plays about monarchs and elected political leaders until the last decade of his writing career. He was always an enemy of big government and of totalitarianism — the one naturally leading to the other, he thought — for he held with Thomas Jefferson and Henry David Thoreau that the less government the better; and he believed that those men who governed for very long eventually wronged both themselves and the governed because something in their system — notably, the temptations offered the ambitious and the ineluctable desire of some to rule others — would permit neither political idealism nor common sense nor humaneness nor true love to prosper. Absolutism is especially open to corruption, reminding us of Lord Acton's famous letter to Bishop Mandell Creighton (April 5, 1887) containing the lines:

. . . I cannot accept your canon that we are to judge Pope and King unlike other men, with a favorable presumption that they did no wrong. If there is any presumption it is the other way against holders of power, increasing as power increases. . . . *Power tends to corrupt and absolute power corrupts absolutely* [italics mine].

I Barefoot in Athens

Barefoot in Athens, completed in 1951 and staged that fall, is based mainly but not exclusively upon Plato's dialogues and Xenophon's *Memorabilia*. It illuminates most entertainingly the final months of Socrates, a figure clearly congenial to the aging Anderson who was himself a latterday gadfly who had suffered several firings for his convictions. In this play, Anderson uses his poetic license to deviate a little not only from his two major sources but, to a

66

lesser extent, even from the implications of his Preface, "Socrates and His Gospel." In this Preface, as well as in "Notes on Socrates" that was printed in the *New York Times*,[1] he makes much ado about finding and reporting the real Socrates of history whom, he says, Plato distorted in his later writings.

Anderson's story of Socrates opens at the time of the Peloponnesian War in the household of the destitute philosopher — the place is represented on the stage by props rather than by sets — where we learn that he is an unworldly yet loving husband and father. He is so indifferent to making money that he refuses payment for his teaching: this obstinate resistance to making money helps account for his wife's shrewish outbursts. Against old Socrates, whose greatest sin seems to have been that he stepped on the tender assumptions of various influential bigots and ignoramuses during his relentless search for truth, a trio of Athenians have brought an indictment charging him with impiety and with corrupting the minds of young men. His enemies are outraged that several of his former pupils who rose to power have subsequently betrayed Athens; the truth is, however, that such pupils willfully strayed from his teachings and failed to inquire also, in their alleged questioning of all things whatsoever, the value of such things as murder, blood money, and illegally gained office.

Before the trial of Socrates can be held, Sparta defeats Athens, the city so beloved by the philosopher, and installs the Thirty Oligarchs under the unscrupulous Critias — the former pupil and the present example of the danger of Socrates' teachings! One of the most vivid and likeable of all the figures in *Barefoot in Athens* is the Spartan king, Pausanias, who learns to admire Socrates and who warns him that the return of democracy to Athens, when it comes, would revive the old charges. Sure enough, after a successful rebellion forces Pausanias and his troops to leave the city, Socrates' enemies bring him to trial, the events of which constitute the high point of the drama. In this section of the play, the tragic flaw of Socrates becomes apparent; it consists of no single fault but a combination of virtue, which has been carried to excess, and several errors of judgment. Socrates is overly confident that he will defeat his accusers in open argument (as if court cases are won or lost simply on the merits of argument); he refuses to make the customary tricky appeals to the mercy of the court; when he skillfully outwits his accusers on some points, he befuddles the jurors who are to pass judgment; he offends the court by saying that his conviction would prove a stain on the reputation of Athens; and, master though he is at debate, he somehow lets himself be trapped into admitting that he loves truth more than Athens — clear proof to the jury of disloyalty. Convicted, he is sentenced to death. Pausanias visits him in jail and offers to provide him freedom and a palace in Sparta, but Socrates cannot bring himself to violate the laws of the city he loves or to trade a democracy, which sometimes errs, for a tyranny where error is standard practice. The play ends as he awaits dawn and his death.

Some of the critics of the play were bothered by the characterization of Socrates, partly because of their misunderstanding of what Anderson had intended there and had actually accomplished, and partly because of their disappointment that he had not emphasized those spiritual and philosophical aspects of Socrates which Plato had covered exceedingly well. John Mason Brown in his review of *Barefoot in Athens* objects to the depiction of Socrates as "a loving father, a loyal Athenian, an ardent democrat" during the death scene rather than as a great and moving philosopher who discourses about the immortality of the soul.[2] What Brown was unfairly requesting was a re-working of what Plato had already accomplished in *Phaedo*. Whereas, the evidence in the play indicates that Anderson wanted to emphasize the human being and the patriot — what the school books, including Plato's writings, treat at best lightly — more than the philosopher; and Anderson was certainly entitled to take this new approach. Moreover, it would have been hypocritical or at least unwise for Anderson to have attempted in that last scene any kind of discourse on the soul's immortality, for he was not convinced that such immortality was possible.[3]

I must agree with Mabel Bailey who claims that the play was not meant to be a drama of ideas,[4] but I qualify my agreement by adding that the question is one of emphasis only, because Socrates' arguments with Critias and especially with Lycon, in Act I, Scene ii, and Act II, Scene ii, respectively, demonstrate clearly a flashing interplay of minds. We have not the space to do justice to Bailey's objections about the stage Socrates — her treatment is relatively long, brilliant in places, yet not altogether convincing — but she does penetrate to the main difficulty, which is that Socrates is unwilling to admit that the Athenian court which convicted him is an example of the corruption of power in a group; moreover, it is "shocking" that he flatters the obviously vengeful jury by attributing to it not only thoughtful deliberation but its *right* to get rid of him when and how it wishes:

What they have is the power. They may abuse their power as other rulers do. But might does not make right in a democracy any more than in a monarchy or a dictatorship. There is no escaping the moral law by recourse to numbers. Power is corrupting, as corrupting to a group as to an individual. But Mr. Anderson cannot bring himself to allow his play to reveal this truth. He has a stake in freedom. He wishes to keep a free people believing in themselves and in their institutions. . . .[5]

No doubt Anderson's reluctance to depict drawbacks in democracy had something to do with the then famous Joseph McCarthy's "witchhunt" hearings in the United States Senate when much of the nation feared that Communists were undermining the Federal government. In the play, Anderson tries to make Athens look good in comparison with supposedly Communistic Sparta (though this explicit identification does not occur in the play itself, but in the Preface). Avery tells us that, after Anderson had finished a version of *Barefoot in Athens*, he then read Karl R. Popper's anti-Plato study *The Open Society and Its Enemies* (the 1943 and 1950 editions were available); and he revised the dramatic work in the light of what he had discovered in Popper.[6] In fact, Anderson's Preface was particularly colored from the reading of this critic. Accordingly, among the things that might have come to Anderson from reading Popper, or reinforced his concepts, is the belief that Socrates' criticism of Athens was a "democratic one, and indeed of the kind that is the very life of democracy" [Popper's words].[7]

However, Jackson K. Hershbell in his essay "The Socrates and Plato of Maxwell Anderson" argues cogently that Anderson's Preface is wrong in representing Sparta as a thoroughgoing Communist state because its actual government was altogether too much a mixture and also too totalitarian for such a simple labeling to be acceptable. Hershbell indicates, moreover, that it was also wrong to present Athens as a thoroughgoing democratic state because slavery existed there, because women and slaves did not have the vote, and because only children whose parents were citizens could receive citizenship.[8] Anderson was on much safer grounds in representing Socrates as a person closer to the heart's desire because the historical Socrates has been the subject of far more widely conflicting in-

terpretations than has been the case with Athens. History, to this
playwright, is the unreliable stuff of which artists' dreams are made.

But Anderson seriously undercuts the ideological message in this
play by having his hero, a champion of democracy, be convicted by a
so-called "democratic" jury and by then omitting to signal satisfac-
torily that there has been a perversion of justice. Furthermore, the
kindest, the most generous, the most perceptive friend other than
Xantippe that Anderson bestows on Socrates is King Pausanias, a
tyrant — a veritable Communist, according to the definition in the
Preface. Anderson clearly has mixed feelings about democracy-in-
action despite his years of patriotic war effort in the 1940's and his
anti-Communist attitude in the Preface to *Barefoot in Athens*; consequently, he cannot help playing the devil's advocate a trifle too
well. He admires the ideal of democracy *as it is advocated and
defended by Socrates*, but he cannot help distrusting and disliking
that ideal as objectified in an actual city state that lawfully liquidates
one of her noblest citizens.

Anderson, like his hero a democratic liberal, supplied the best
criticism to date on the advantages and limitations of his Socrates'
mode of skeptical inquiry. This criticism is found in his "Notes for
Barefoot in Athens" that lies buried in box #twenty-two of the
papers of The Playwrights' Producing Company. Paraphrased, it
runs: In examining the basis of morality, one can destroy that morality [as Anderson's Socrates helped to do]; no faith can withstand
examination, any more than a tree can live if its roots are exposed;
and yet, paradoxically, there is freedom only when man constantly
examines life, unhampered by external restraints and restrictions.
Thus we exist on the horns of this dilemma: to examine means life,
but it can also mean death; it embodies both and all the inter-
mediate tension.[9] In contemporary parlance, then, Anderson admitted that the choice between individual liberty and national security
remained an urgent but unsolved problem for him during the Cold
War period. His drama could only raise the problem; no answer was
possible.[10]

The characterization of Socrates is not, however, completely inef-
fective. He is drawn quite humanly with a credible touch of the
erotic (as in Plato), with an easy-going conviviality, and with the
quaint habit of going barefoot[11] although he is willing to don his
sandals temporarily before passing a playground where his child
might otherwise be embarrassed. Hardly anyone could quarrel with

the portrayal of Pausanias, who is amusing though murderous, who was a real person active in Piraeus and Athens in 403 B.C. when the Athenian democrats overthrew the Thirty Oligarchs and chased out the Spartans.[12] Yet his offer to rescue Socrates is strictly a product of Anderson's imagination. Also imaginary is the placing of the 403 B.C. revolt and the 399 B.C. trial of Socrates within a few weeks of each other; but such compression helps to give the play unity. Theodote is probably an invention, suggested by the *hetairai* who must have been present at some of the drinking discussions in which Plato had his Socrates participate. Xantippe, whom tradition describes as a shrew, is in this work a loving, amazingly loyal wife whose disagreeableness is plausibly explained by the grinding effects of poverty.

The first stage enactment failed quickly; and for this failure George Jean Nathan, Brooks Atkinson, Walter Kerr, and John Gassner put much of the blame on the acting and directing. The failure of *Barefoot in Athens* — The Playwrights' Producing Company lost seventy thousand dollars on the production — threw Anderson into such deep despair that he resolved not to write any more plays for Broadway as long as Brooks Atkinson remained a critic; he lamented that the current stage had no demand anymore for serious work: only for shock, sex, or insipid musicals.[13] Although we recognize that *Barefoot in Athens* has several faults, we also think it deserves more attention than the critics and public have usually given it.

II   The Golden Six

The setting now shifts from the Greek court to the Roman palace where we see this time the corruption of absolute power. Anderson must have known how a government, once committed to a misguided course of policy, perversely rejects all change; and he could hardly help finding in the scandalous succession of Roman emperors a subject guaranteed to point up some heavy moral. The story in *The Golden Six* tells of the rise and fall of Roman emperors from Augustus to Claudius, but it is also a chronicle that reflects the author's pessimism about the disparity between a people's desire for freedom in government and what they feel impelled to accept and perpetuate once tyranny has begun. Technically, the structure of *The Golden Six* is reminiscent of *Anne of the Thousand Days* in that

the principal character, the Emperor Claudius, first presented in
solitude as the curtain rises, recounts in the subsequent story what
he has lived through; Claudius here differs from Henry VIII in that
he keeps his thoughts in a diary.

Claudius hopes his diary, which records his frustrations and disillusionment, will assist those distant men of the future who attempt
to establish free government; but he believes there is scarcely any
chance for freedom to endure in a world in which someone will
always seek to dominate others. Through his eyes, so to speak, we
learn about the Empress Livia, the wife of Augustus, who connives
and poisons so that only her favorites are among those who are in
succession to the throne; however, her chosen people are usually
degenerate; and she is always the real power behind the perverts.
But much to Livia's chagrin and to Claudius' own sincere disappointment, the latter finally becomes emperor near the end of the
story but feels helpless then about changing the cruel system he has
inherited. However, the theater audience cannot help wondering
how such impotence can exist since now the new emperor has the
enormous power needed to implement any number of reforms. The
dramatist, on the other hand, wants us to believe that Claudius
embodies the tragedy of the good man who, despite his having had
excellent reasons for condemning tyranny, is compelled against his
will to head precisely that kind of regime.[14]

Though Claudius is ostensibly the hero, almost everything about
him is so wooden that we are likely to treat him with the same
contempt and pity that almost all the play's characters have for him!
Livia is easily the more interesting character since *she* is not
paralyzed in imagination and will; cunningly malignant, she also has
the courage to get things done and undone. The main trouble with
the play is that the theater audience is supposed to believe against
its will that, even with the benign Claudius at last in charge, no
appreciable good can arise; that the empire will continue to grind on
inhumanly because of a defect in man (the compulsion to rule
others); and that man in his search for freedom is almost certainly
doomed to failure. Absent is any feeling of tragic exaltation in *The
Golden Six;* nowhere is there a temptation for us to pause, as with
Hamlet, and marvel at what a wondrous creature man is — at least
on a scale of potentiality. Incidentally, Anderson omits to employ in
this work one of his rules governing serious drama, specifically rule
three (the protagonist, representative of the forces of good, must

win); in consequence of which it is rather difficult to empathize with Claudius, whose role in history is made here to seem futile and unmanly. Like Prince Rudolph in *The Masque of Kings*, he does not have that heroic stature necessary to change a malign system of government even the tiniest bit toward the better.

Anderson's ill health at the time of his writing this play no doubt contributed to the more intense pessimism and to the general drop in dramatic quality.[15] This tired drama never reached a Broadway audience in the author's lifetime; instead, it ran in the off-Broadway York Playhouse in 1958 using a largely undistinguished cast. Not even the advertisements of semi-nudity upon the stage — a lovely slave girl disrobes several times — could lure customers to more than seventeen performances.

III   Joan of Lorraine

In the world of Andersonia, the corruption of power indigenous to the Athenian court and to the succession of Roman emperors continues on into the Middle Ages with both church and state, as we can see next in *Joan of Lorraine*. In a 1946 article for the *New York Times*, Anderson spoke of two main reasons for putting together his drama about the great French national heroine; one of these reasons has to do with dramatic technique, the other with theme. He said that his reason for using the play-within-a-play device was that he had always wanted to have a theater audience participate in the excitement he himself had often felt in watching a play blossom into life during rehearsal. Additionally, he wanted to explore the problem of faith — of what a man can believe in a world of disillusionment and power politics.[16] Although Anderson does not say so in his article, he must have been motivated in this play which he began writing in 1944[17] by his attitude toward the conflict inherent in America's prosecution of World War II — namely, a conflict in which America, the announced champion of democratic freedom, had found it expedient for the defeat of the Axis powers to join forces with a totalitarian regime that Anderson greatly feared, Communist Russia.

The setting for the two-act *Joan of Lorraine* is a Broadway theater where a director (Masters), who is harassed by practical problems that necessitate compromises if the play is ever to open, is rehearsing his cast for a drama about Joan of Arc. During interludes in the rehearsals, the leading lady, Mary Grey, complains to director Masters about the way the absentee author is re-writing the script to show the heroine as willing to compromise with evil people — such as the dauphin — in order to obey thereby the behests of her "voices." In this conviction Mary differs sharply from Masters, who holds that such an idealistic person as Joan *must* enlist the aid of some people of bad character who are "running things," if any of her goals are to be gained; and, to prove his view, he cites realistic examples of such a necessity from show business. Masters is clearly a *persona* for Maxwell Anderson himself; for both men are doggedly idealistic, are distrustful of public leaders, are skeptical of established religions and yet unwilling to part with them, and are filled with a belief in the theater as democracy's temple (Act II, Rehearsal Preface).

The close of Act I marks a high point of tension when Mary is so frustrated at the way Joan's role now stands that she walks out for a lunch break from which, she hints, she might not bother to return. In a sense, then, two Joans have emerged thus far in *Joan of Lorraine;* and each of them will have to re-examine the basis of her faith before she can continue to pursue an idealistic course of conduct. But Mary does return to the stage after lunch. And, in acting out the prison scene, she discovers from her portrayal of Joan, who recants her confession and re-affirms a faith in her "voices," that she can continue to act the play as it is now written. Mary is at last in agreement with Masters that her heroine, Joan, would occasionally stoop to compromise on little things in order to achieve her aims, but she would dare even being burned to death before compromising her soul.[18]

Although Anderson clearly spent a longer time on *Joan of Lorraine* than he did on any other drama (he was two years at the task),[19] although he used as noble a theme as may be found anywhere in literature, and although he followed closely his theory of tragedy in writing the play, the resultant work is still not among his best. The substance — however we may admire Anderson's intentions — seems thinner than it should be in a treatment of such an amazing historical personage — the very stuff of which epics are made. Of course, the interludes with their behind-the-scenes theater business are sure to interest most readers and theatergoers — who have a natural curiosity about such experience — but the story of Joan is at least equally intriguing and seems to cry out for fully-arranged sets and costumes and, yes, uninterrupted action. The interludes, moreover, continually remind us as we go along that all is mere playacting. Thus verisimilitude suffers a little at the expense of gaining a clever subplot that parallels the main one, even though this subplot is worthwhile in indicating the everlasting relevancy of past and current ethical problems.

Comparisons with G. B. Shaw's more famous *Saint Joan* of an earlier era are almost inevitable. Shaw's Joan hears "voices" too, but they originate in her head and represent common sense; she is a disarmingly frank and even witty girl; a fire-breathing revolutionary eager for battle and unmindful of the cost in casualties, she finds things "dull! dull! dull!" when danger is past. Anderson's Joan, on the other hand, hears "voices" that are divinely inspired; she is a shy, feminine, modest, and home-loving girl who goes strongly against her natural impulses in following a martial life; in battle, she weeps over the death of so many fallen troops on both sides. In some ways, therefore, she is a much more believable person as a martyr and woman than Shaw's Joan — but Anderson's heroine is less interesting as a unique personality, or as a heroine fit for high deeds of a masculine order. The judges in the Shavian work are reasonable, if spiritually misguided, men who go out of their way to save the girl's body and soul; in Anderson's work, they are bigoted and evil, cruel and vindictive — and, hence, more in line with the general verdict of history. Charles in Shaw's *Saint Joan* grows from a petulant coward into something almost resembling a man, thanks to Joan's good offices; for, after having neglected to rescue her from her captors, he years later congratulates himself for having rehabilitated her name — after she is safely dead. In *Joan of Lorraine*, he is from first to last a weak, licentious, ungrateful scoundrel and coward; and he is essentially unchanged by his contact with the saint's life.

In view of the need to communicate to the audience as much as possible of the poetic atmosphere in *Joan of Lorraine*, Anderson was wise in selecting the fine actress Ingrid Bergman as his star; because many of the reviewers of the New York production, which opened for a long run on November 18, 1946, credited much of the play's popularity to her magnificent interpretation. But the reviews were generally mixed. To Eric Bentley, the frame technique, praised by some critics, was not actually original and amounted to a talking down to the audience by preaching so directly to it.[20] J. W. Krutch blasted the work as a whole as "something which could, with uncomfortable accuracy, be described as Shaw and water."[21] Later commentators such as Allardyce Nicoll and John Gassner have for the most part not treated the play kindly, and others have given it only faint support.

IV   Anne of the Thousand Days

In turning from a perusal of *Joan of Lorraine* to this play we are confronted with a distinct rise in literary quality. As the first in the Tudor verse trilogy, *Anne of the Thousand Days* (1948) describes the conflict of political power and sexual passion in the lives of Henry VIII and Anne Boleyn until her execution in 1536 on a charge of adultery.[22] Each of the three stylized acts begins with a monologue spoken, successively, by Anne, Henry, and Anne, who are responsible for the story material in those respective acts in the sense that all the action on stage consists of recollections in their minds. We have here a poetic memory play whose two leading characters are more complex, if far less likeable, than Masters and Mary in *Joan of Lorraine;* moreover, in this new play the technical method of shifting scene from one character to another does not detract from verisimilitude. Although curtains separate the acts, the scenes themselves shift by means of lighting arrangements: the old action is darkened out when a new one is illuminated on a different part of the stage.

As the curtain rises on the prologue to Act I, we see Anne on the evening before her execution sitting in the Tower of London where she recalls some of the thousand days that have passed since she first gave herself to Henry. Her mood is by turns sensual, proud, and meditative — and they are quite in keeping with what we learn about her chameleon personality as the play continues. In her memory, young King Henry, lusting for a new royal wench, visits again the household of his treasurer Thomas Boleyn in order to woo the saucy Anne Boleyn, whose married sister he had already made pregnant. Anne resists him at first because she is passionately in love with the Earl of Northumberland; but Cardinal Wolsey, the unconscionable procurer for His Majesty, breaks up the match and warns that, unless she submits, Northumberland as well as her own family will hurt for it. Whereupon her spineless parents, who are already in debt to Henry for royal favors, begin to urge Anne to compromise herself.

Anne, who is smart and ambitious enough to hold out for marriage, finally has her will; but there is a *secret* marriage because he is still encumbered with Queen Katharine. Anne, now pregnant by him, soon grows impatient and insists that he get the divorce immediately so that her child will be legitimate and can succeed to the throne. Since the Pope will not grant a divorce, Cromwell, secretary to Wolsey, points out to Henry that he can achieve his marriage to Anne and also enormous wealth by looting the rich monasteries if he will but make himself the head of the church in England. After Henry has done so, Anne upsets his plans for succession by bearing him a daughter. Finally, Anne becomes queen and then takes advantage of her position by getting enmeshed in the evils of power play which beset various Anderson heroines and heroes who rise to the purple; for she demands that Henry execute Sir Thomas More and any others who refuse to recognize the Act of Succession which would guarantee the infant Elizabeth's eventual title to the crown. Then intrigue begins against her as Henry's evil genius, Cromwell, playing on the king's desire to be rid of Anne, fabricates evidence of her adultery so that Henry will have to order her arrest and trial. A court finds her guilty and sentences her to the block.

The portrait of Anne is both internally consistent and convincing. In devising her as a tragic figure, Maxwell Anderson followed Aristotle's recipe in that Anne is a person of high station who is initially neither faultless nor corrupt, who suffers *hamartia* (in Anne's case, errors of judgment), who undergoes a recognition phase (Act III, Scene iv) and admits her guilt for slaughtering innocent people, who then wants the expiation of death, and who at last goes down to defeat. She also has the trait common to all tragic figures — courage, one of the rarest and most admirable human qualities. Anne has both great strengths and great weaknesses; and given the situations in which she is placed — notably the temptations afforded by queenly power — her conduct is wholly believable. So skillfully was she wrought as a stage figure that some of her very strengths, her pride and passionate dedication to the welfare of her child plus her quite human desire to keep that child from being declared a bastard, become precisely the means for her catastrophe.

And so, Anne's choosing to die was more than just an expiation (after the trial Henry offered her exile in return for a marriage annulment), because her death amounted to a praiseworthy sacrifice for her daughter's sake. This dramatic technique of felling the hero or heroine by means of her own virtue underlies, of course, many of the most outstanding tragedies in Western civilization. John Webster in *The Duchess of Malfi* put it this way: "Whether we fall by ambition, blood, or lust, / Like diamonds, we are cut down with our own dust" (Act V, Scene v). Anderson gives quite a few effective touches to his heroine, and he makes us feel that in Anne's death justice will be done. For example, as she is waiting in the Tower to die, we are made to participate in the horror of her predicament when she remembers the story of More's daughter who climbed up the trestles of London Bridge to recover the gory head of her father from a spike and take it home for secret burial.

Anderson described his Henry VIII as the "Sexual Everyman" whose excesses resulted not from increased lust but from unusual temptations.[23] This view is a surprisingly charitable one of a young man who, if we are to believe Anne in the play, had fathered at least a dozen children, legitimate and otherwise, by the time that he met her; and who, before he died, had a total of six wives, not counting mistresses that he never wed, in his avowed search for a legitimate male heir. Henry's daily prayers to God and his conceited belief that what he does is God's will do not by any means prevent him from playing Zeus to every Leda that he meets; the mere sight of a maid was almost sure to arouse his dynastic urge. In Act I, Scene i, he plainly announces that to him love is simply physical, the assuaging of painful desire. In his rutting courtship with Anne, he is so uninhibited that he greedily possesses her anywhere!

But Henry is much more than a lusty monarch; Anderson gives him a depth of character that is unknown among the phantoms who drift through *The Golden Six*. In Act II, Scene ii, at that point in the action where Henry is launched upon his course of political evil in a way that makes his previous transgressions appear to have been the merest trifles — now he has obeyed Anne and ordered some of his old friends executed — he is struck by the disparity between his earlier idealism and innocence that had inspired him to write a love poem, and his wicked actions that have been committed for the sake of his ambitious new queen. Here we glimpse Henry as a confused soul well lost — a selfish man drawn into evil because of his desire to please his consort, his need for a male heir, and his rapacity for the riches of Catholic properties. One of the most poetic and memorable parts of this verse play appears in the monologue beginning "There is a load every man lugs behind him," for Henry reveals in it the unrest of his conscience (Act II, Scene iv). Once upon a time in the full moon of their new-found love, Anne had expressed the belief that he would become a truly great king; perhaps she was impressed by the richness of his endowments — musician, scholar, linguist, and athlete — but her final estimate of him is devastating in its brevity and pointedness: to wit, that even a coroner now could not discover that Henry had already, for all intents and purposes, died young (Act III, Scene iv).

In *Anne of the Thousand Days*, Maxwell Anderson takes a few liberties with English history. For instance, he depicts Anne as being as much sinned against as sinning and as having been a more physically attractive person than was the historical Anne of the wide mouth, long neck, and swarthy complexion. In the script, we never doubt that she is innocent of the adultery charged against her; but the case in history remains unproved although numerous responsible parties, including her own uncle and father, attested to or concurred in her guilt. Of Henry's military exploits and timely strengthening of the royal navy Anderson properly says nothing. Since Anderson in reality had no love for him,[24] what he presents about Henry is consistent with the ogre of history: he is a brutal egotist who happens to discover that the desires of his kingdom (toward independence from Rome) coincide with his own selfish bent for riches and power. Among the several probably deliberate anachronisms that occur in this drama, one is that the real Wolsey was dead before Henry had completed his futile negotiations with the Pope concerning a divorce; therefore Anne could not have banished him nor could Henry have executed him after their marriage.[25] Incidentally, the song "Waking at night . . ." that is sung by Henry (Act II, Scene ii) is an original by Anderson himself, and it is markedly superior to the song material in Act I, Scene iv, that was composed by the real Henry and that was combined into one song by Anderson.[26]

The first Broadway production, starring Rex Harrison and Joyce Redman in the lead roles, began in December, 1948; and it ran for 226 performances and was a resounding commercial success. Nonetheless, Harold Clurman opined that the actors and the settings did not do justice to Anderson's art and that, by and large,

"The effect of all . . . is a fundamental dryness."[27] When J. M. Brown called the work "serviceable enough as theater," he was surely making an understatement; for Brooks Atkinson described it glowingly (and more accurately) as a "passionate chronicle . . . . No one else has the strength to write on this theatrical level and use the stage with such abandon."[28]

A libel suit spoiled Anderson's pleasure with his successful play. Francis Hackett, the Irish author of the novels *Henry the Eighth* (1929), of *Queen Anne Boleyn* (1938), and of a then unpublished dramatization of the latter work, soon charged in a newspaper statement that Anderson had plagiarized from his first book. Anderson, outraged, countered with a hundred thousand dollar libel suit and entered evidence from his diary to trace his play up to its final form as an original work. In Anderson's unofficial public defense that he presented in "How a Play Gets Written: Diary Retraces the Steps" in the *New York Herald Tribune* during August, 1949, he admits that in late 1947 he had read not only Hackett's *Henry the Eighth* but other books such as Edith Sitwell's *Fanfare for Elizabeth* and Martin Hume's *The Wives of Henry the Eighth;* but he expresses no acknowledged indebtedness to any of these items: Hackett's work was lost in a mélange of readings. Within a few days after having read Hume, he had conceived the idea of having the whole story consist of recollected scenes that would create a Henry who was a symbol of animal man.[29] In a letter dated May, 1949, to John Wharton of The Playwrights' Producing Company, Anderson defends himself by declaring that *nowhere* does Hackett in his book convey the whole action as occurring within the minds of the main characters. This particular technique meant everything to the dramaturgist. Hackett finally dropped his own suit when Anderson agreed to pay him one dollar in charges.[30]

V   Mary of Scotland

Mary, Queen of Scots, was another British monarch to go down in the contest for imperial power. She has intrigued any number of literary artists from Johann von Schiller's *Mary Stuart* (1800) to Robert Bolt's *Vivat! Vivat Regina!* (1970). Whether Anderson had read or was influenced by any of the literary accounts, I have been unable to determine, though I suspect that he read many. But it is easy to see that when he formed his story about Mary, many of the accepted facts of history went off on vacation. The then shortest actress on the American stage, Helen Hayes, who claims that he wrote the part for her, was at first distressed about portraying one of history's tallest queens until Anderson consoled her in the following manner: " 'You're not playing that woman, you're playing my version of her. So, don't obscure, don't fuzz up my vision of her by reading other people's' " biographies of this queen.[31] Not surprisingly, Anderson's Mary and Bothwell are exceedingly Romanticized. In his version are absent, among other things, the real Mary's forced abdication of the throne even while she was still in Scotland and also her divorce from Bothwell. Though the real Bothwell had a wife at the time he wanted to wed Mary, no one in the play mentions the wife; nor is there any hint of his adultery with a maidservant during his first marriage, although Anderson does represent him as a lecher. Not merely are the two principals altered to make them — especially Mary — seem admirable as well as victims of Machiavellian politics, but minor aspects of the reign are discarded and others are so transformed that the actual seven years can be compressed into the seemingly short time necessary for staging.[32]

The opening scene of this three-act play[33] shows Mary Stuart arriving on a windy, sleety pier in Scotland, but only her admirer the loyal and outspoken Earl of Bothwell greets her as she, a Catholic, begins her troublesome reign over a largely Protestant kingdom in which many subjects hate her despite her personal beauty, graciousness, and gentle ways. This scene not only prefigures much of the play but is such a theatrical triumph in mood setting and character delineation that Anderson was never to surpass it. Our heart goes out immediately to Mary; and we are not surprised that even the Protestant fanatic Knox, who greets her with rude obscenity, successively mollifies his terms of address until he calls her "Your Majesty" — and even kisses her hand. What charisma for a queen!

A short time later, Queen Elizabeth plots in England with Lord Burghley to bring about Mary's downfall through craft; for she believes, or pretends to believe, that Mary will challenge her right to the English throne. Also, Elizabeth has reason to fear Mary's Catholic connections in France. Burghley, who urges these purely *political* considerations, unwittingly provides a cover for Elizabeth's real motives. Her consciously evil plan is to undermine the Scottish queen's reputation among her own subjects by spreading vicious gossip and lies; moreover, she will contrive to marry her to a fool, the Catholic Darnley, heir next after Mary to the English throne, a match sure to set the Protestant Scots against their queen.

Yet, as noted earlier, political rivalry is not Elizabeth's main consideration: she is clearly jealous of the great personal charm and noble spirit of her rival, of her recently-won popularity as a regent who is presumptuous and naive enough to believe that she can run a country without having to sacrifice, as the cynical Elizabeth did, her devotion to honor, truth, and justice. There is nothing like popular virtue to raise envy and therefore hatred in malignant souls. Probably what Elizabeth resents especially is the spectacle of the good heart succeeding where cold craft ought by rights to be triumphant! And she will perpetrate her deviltry with impunity, because history, she congratulates herself, will remember not that she brought a lovely queen to ruin, but only that she was queen of England and ruled well. [34]

At this juncture, we respond with an electric shudder, knowing that history has perhaps played us false — and Elizabeth later remarks in Act III that all history is forgery — that here is the *real* Bess stripped of the public relations mask with which tradition has beguiled us. The remaining events in the play show the diabolical scheme unfolding with lethal sureness. Mary rejects her true love, Bothwell, in order to marry Darnley (and spite Elizabeth, she supposes); and soon she regrets her marriage, the more so when Darnley proves a sot and contrives the murder of her faithful secretary; then Darnley is himself murdered. Finally, Mary is forced to flee to England where, ironically, she becomes a prisoner of the Elizabeth from whom she had fully expected aid and refuge.

In an exceptionally moving encounter between the two queens — one which never happened in history — Mary hears the poisonous truth from her rival's own lips. She learns that Elizabeth, too, came to the throne loving truth (she said), but years of shuffling politics changed her into one who gave up good faith and learned to love only where her material interest lay (Act III). Mary can go free if only she will sign an abdication; but she refuses, trusting to posterity to restore her reputation. Her enemy then tries to disillusion her by insinuating, like the Communists, that history is merely what people believe, and that she will take care to mold those beliefs. However, Mary remains undaunted by this threat and by the prospect of years of privation and solitude that await her in confinement; and she rises as morally superior to her plight in the drama's brilliant climax. We are left to conclude that Mary's tragic flaw consists in believing she can play out the game of power politics without sullying her immortal soul. After she attempts what Anderson seems to believe is impossible, she remains unsullied but suffers defeat because her political enemies, who are blind to all moral niceties, entrap the good Mary in her own virtue. Like Lord Essex in another play, Mary is duly warned; but she allows her pride to lead her into the trap set by her enemies; and, like him in defeat, she refuses the offer of personal freedom in exchange for her ideals.

The poetry expressed in the final scene and elsewhere in the drama is so severe and so crystal clear that it avoids the turgidity that sometimes mars Anderson's endeavors; nonetheless, it offers hardly a single memorable line that is striking in imagery. This lack is owing to Anderson's slow development as a dramatic poet: he had two more years to go before, in *Winterset*, he ripened his lyric powers and made a music commensurate with his high conception of tragedy; before that time, apparently needing assurance, he restrained his verse until he could meet with a favorable public response to poetic drama.

In the first Broadway production, which ran for 248 performances, Anderson fortunately had the talents of the excellent actors Helen Hayes, Helen Menken, and Philip Merivale in the roles of Mary, Elizabeth, and Bothwell, respectively. The gifted Robert Edmond Jones designed the sets. The best historical drama yet composed by an American, was what John Mason Brown wrote in his review. Edith J. R. Isaacs confirmed this applause: "[It] is the best . . . he has written, the finest poetry, the clearest, most luminous characterizations [thus far]"[35] What the first-night audiences saw at the Alvin Theatre on November 27, 1933, when the curtain rose on *Mary of Scotland* was the first Anderson verse play to fully use his theory of tragedy. The most noticeable features of this development, as differentiated from his previous treatments, are that the protagonist has a recognition scene (in Act III of the present work) and in consequence becomes a morally better person. True to the additional requirements laid down in "The Essence of Tragedy"

(p. 8), this episode is central to the play, and everything else is subordinate to it. The big question, argued heatedly by some critics, is whether this formalism proved harmful in *Mary of Scotland*.

John Gassner holds that all of the history plays written according to the tragic formula were harmed somewhat, save for *Anne of the Thousand Days*,[36] though I cannot understand the basis for his contention. A more reasonable assessment comes from Arthur M. Sampley, who shows convincingly that the formula of "weakness followed by self-discovery" that is used so often by Anderson is not a fault in itself (i.e., does not alone account for the playwright's failures any more than it alone accounts for his successes) but that he wrote best when he went beyond the formula. In other words, Anderson's announced criteria for tragedy neglected to include some crucial elements that he used to advantage in better works than *Mary of Scotland* — namely, in *Winterset* and *High Tor*. Thus his formula helped only when used in conjunction with a greater complexity of characterization than had been the case in most of the pre-1935 works. The formula and such characterization led to fictional people who are rich and memorable in themselves and to a finer poetry than he had hitherto used because he was not "chary of imaginative ornament or of too pronounced a rhythm."[37]

But *Mary of Scotland*, good though it is, does not represent this great leap forward in artistry. Though formed later than *Elizabeth the Queen*, the characterizations are actually simpler, melodramatically so, in order to lend emphasis to the polarities of good and evil that might otherwise escape the reader brought up on the myth of Queen Elizabeth's unalloyed virtues. In seeing the figures reduced to a black-and-white status, the reader is likely to conclude, however, that the author protests too much. The drama is, nonetheless, entertaining and thought-provoking; and, in this respect, it is not far below vintage Anderson. Mary is all the more personable and admirable in our eyes because she is the noble victim of a conspiracy, because she does not stoop to do evil just because evil is done to her, and because she does not make war on her enemies (as Bothwell advises) rather than try to win them over by fair and gentle womanly treatment.

Still, she is not too good to be true as a realistically conceived character, regardless of Anderson's almost wholesale departures from what passes now as historical fact. Of course, Anderson is not the first to treat her so benignly since Schiller and others made her a loveable martyr and Elizabeth a beast. *Mary of Scotland* shares with other works by the dramatist the idea that the morally sensitive and idealistic person will go down crushed beneath the heel of the political realist, of which there is never any shortage in the royal courts of Andersonia. Like other plays of his — even the most serious — this one is relaxed enough here and there to indulge in a charming wit. Perhaps the best single example of the latter occurs in Act II, Scene i, where Knox, after haughtily addressing Mary in his customary sulphurously Biblical tones, assures her that he comes to visit her as God's own spokesman; and she responds to this statement that, if his exalted claim were so, then he should show her his divine commission.

VI   Elizabeth the Queen

Although *Elizabeth the Queen* (1930) is preparatory to *Mary of Scotland* with regard to the development of Anderson's tragic formula, the historical era in the play is later by some three decades, with Elizabeth now an old woman. As Anderson's first artistically successful poetic drama to be acted by professionals, *Elizabeth the Queen*, like the other play, uses an exceedingly loose blank verse intermixed with some prose. The general effect is distinctly modern, even though the drama has all the necessary color and atmosphere of a period work. Once the reader or theatergoer is well into the first scene in which Sir Robert Cecil and Sir Walter Raleigh begin to plot against their rival Lord Essex, the dramatic tension never slackens; he is taken into the most splendid age of English history for a thrilling chronicle of the conflict between royal love and the lust for power, presented on a scale rarely seen in American drama. Cecil and Raleigh, jealous of Essex's influence with the elderly queen whom he loves passionately and recklessly, suspect that he is at heart a rebel and plan to lure him into accepting a generalship in Ireland where he can be made to look like a rebel indeed and bring himself to ruin. Essex's nominal supporter Francis Bacon cautions the handsome Essex against his headstrong drive for power — military and regal — and tells him prophetically that, though the queen loves him, she will not permit one of her subjects to eclipse her position. Elizabeth even tells Essex directly that he is more of a "poet" than a general; and that, if he had his way, reckless male chauvinist that he is, he would embroil England in expensive and needless wars in Spain and Flanders.

In the queen's council, the plotters succeed completely with their design to send Essex to Ireland. Before Essex leaves, Elizabeth hands him her father's ring; and she tells him that, when he presents it to her, she will forgive him anything. After Essex is in Ireland and is engaged in his hopeless campaign, his enemies have his mail with Elizabeth intercepted — with disastrous political consequences. The queen, soon frantic and worried at not receiving any letters from him, cannot help believing some of the rumors that he has allied himself with the Irish forces. She questions the crafty Bacon, who has discovered the facts of the intrigue and now wants to play both sides of the affair; but she receives disingenuous answers from him. Driven to desperation and to suspect designs on the throne, she orders Essex to disband his army and return. Essex, stung by her command, arrives at London with his troops and seizes the palace; there, he and the captive queen quickly discover the treachery that has been practiced upon them. But they do so too late for reconciliation: he is more intent on power than ever, and she is still reluctant to share power or relinquish one jot of the imperial role. But, by promising a joint rulership, Elizabeth tricks him into dismissing his palace guard; once in control again, she coldly informs Essex she has learned from trusting him that whoever rules must be altogether friendless, without love or mercy — whereupon she instantly orders his arrest.

The third and final act of the play is just as gripping but in a more anguishing manner because Elizabeth waits during the final hour before Essex's execution for him to send the ring or to beg forgiveness. A presentation of Falstaff scenes from *Henry IV, Part One* fails to entertain her. Tormented by waiting, she orders his appearance. But he proves still too proud to beg; moreover, he says he has learned something about himself, a dreadful truth: were he to be pardoned, he would most certainly try to seize the throne again, notwithstanding all his love for the queen, and would end by destroying the kingdom. Therefore, it is better for him to die young and untarnished than to grow old and be a poor ruler. As he walks off to the headsman, she breaks down in a moment of weakness and freely offers him the scepter; but he pretends not to hear her and walks on. At this crisis in the play, when we admire him unreserv-

edly for the honesty of his self-insight and for his astonishing courage to do the only fitting thing, Essex arrives at his true heroic
stature; and Elizabeth, now queen of emptiness and death, is left
inconsolable with her terrible grief. Indeed, as she has observed
earlier about how Raleigh and Cecil have caused her golden Essex
to over-reach himself, "the rats inherit the earth" (Act III).

If the Elizabeth of history never seemed quite believable in her
variety and contradictoriness — her shrewdness in council, yet her
indifference to the warnings of advisers; her brilliance and her un-
predictability; her rough yet honeyed tongue; her age-defying
seductiveness and her beauty; her unwillingness to give herself a
master despite the passions of the blood — Anderson's drama contains more than enough to convince the skeptic. Everything is made
so clear in *Elizabeth the Queen* that it is as if the great Bess herself
were resurrected. Still, however, she is no more a "virgin queen" in
this account that she is in the usually reliable one by Lytton
Strachey, whose book[38] several commentators have suggested as the
major source of Anderson's character portraits. According to
Maurice Zolotow, Anderson admitted that his source of inspiration
was Strachey but later gave a different version, *viz.* that he had for
many years brooded about Queen Elizabeth.[39]

In considering how the contents of Anderson's play differ from
what is known in the historical records, as well as in the colorful
Strachean version, we find the following differences between fact
and fiction. First, the real Burghley, a minor figure in the drama,
was already in his grave before the time of Essex's Irish campaign.
Second, Essex's 1590 marriage to Frances Walsinghim, the widow
of Sir Philip Sidney, is unmentioned in the drama. Third, all
Elizabethan speech, including the *thee's* and *thou's*, is modernized
into a kind of blank verse line. Fourth, Elizabeth was actually
alarmed at the London uprising, but she has coolness about it in the
play. Fifth, her only recorded wavering after the trial came in a
message from her that the execution should be postponed; the next
day, she ordered that it should go on as planned. Sixth, Essex, after
being condemned, tried unsuccessfully a number of times to save
himself, even at the risk of getting England involved in war with
Scotland; and this treasonable activity is not mentioned in the
drama. Seventh, he *did* send the ring to Elizabeth, according to a
tale which Strachey reports but does not believe; in this tale, the
ring fell by mistake into Lady Nottingham's hands, who kept it

without telling Elizabeth — an incident which, if used in *Elizabeth the Queen*, would have detracted from the tragedy and created melodrama. Eighth, the meeting between Essex and Elizabeth in the last act of the play never occurred in history — she never saw him again after his confinement in the Tower — but the part is dramatically effective in allowing the principals to make the heartbreaking discovery that they must sacrifice their personal desires in order to preserve the empire.[40] All of these changes indicate how readily Anderson ignores history in his desire to tell a good story and in that sense makes *Elizabeth the Queen* all the more original.[41]

We can see that Anderson's tragic theory does not apply fully in this work because Elizabeth, the protagonist, does not after her recognition scene in Act II, Scene iii, develop into a morally better person — she becomes a more efficient political animal, yes, but Anderson clearly does not value that change. Actually, she is bitter, loveless, deeply cynical, and convinced that no one can die happy. But the secondary figure, Essex, does qualify as a tragic hero according to the author's definition: he learns to value true love and his country's welfare above his own reckless and selfish ambition.[42] Although it was three years later that Anderson's tragic theory was fully developed in *Mary of Scotland*, his *Elizabeth the Queen* is nevertheless pivotal in expressing several attitudes found in his other and later works. First and uppermost, Anderson's distrust of power politics and government itself is present; second, he includes his belief that nobler souls are apt to be destroyed by the grubbers after power (in fact, by the pursuit of power itself); and, third, we find his belief that the fit subjects of tragedy are strong personalities, usually but not always from history, brimming with passion and desire; that they fail somehow and suffer mightily for it; and that their response to failure reveals the glory of the human condition and provides what one critic has called a "cross ventilation" of the soul which constitutes the tragic experience.

Thanks to Anderson's reading in Shakespeare, the dialogue of *Elizabeth the Queen* abounds with puns, such as the grave one by Essex where he warns that the headsman is to come for him "sharp on the hour." He also uses the play-within-a-play technique found in Shakespeare to provide a comic interlude for this tragedy. And there is even a fool to entertain; like Lear's fool, this one makes pointed comments about the mistakes of the sovereign; moreover, he is more functional than that other one inasmuch as he has a hopeless love dalliance with Penelope, the queen's lady-in-waiting. And, when we hear Elizabeth greet Essex with "Ill-met by moonlight," we are reminded of Titania and Oberon in *A Midsummer Night's Dream.* Perhaps stung by some critics' objections, Anderson made little use of Shakespearean influence in his following Tudor dramas, but his detractors had caught the scent early and have never ceased hounding him for his early dazzling assimilations which are, incidentally, quite agreeable to all but the most finicky tastes.

The New York City stage performance was, for the most part, a winner with the critics. Stark Young, Alexander Woollcott, John Hutchens, and others wrote about it favorably. Anita Block reports that audiences, who of course knew little or nothing about Anderson's transformations of history and his almost unheard of desire to ennoble the modern stage with poetic tragedy, discussed the merits of the drama mainly with respect to Lynn Fontanne's makeup as the aging monarch. [43] Unfortunately, some later scholarly commentators have been no more perceptive about the work than were those audiences; for such critics give a disproportionate attention to Anderson's "imitativeness" of style; moreover, they suppose, without warrant, that many or most other Anderson plays are similarly and unashamedly mortgaged to the Bard — almost as if to write history plays in any form of blank verse is *ipse facto* Shakespearean.

VII   Knickerbocker Holiday

The tremendous versatility of Anderson's talent is nowhere more apparent than in his ability to write moving tragedy about the imperial struggles of kings and queens and then turn easily to rollicking satire about, in the present instance, some pretentious Dutch burghers of the New World who figure in *Knickerbocker Holiday.* His intellectual curiosity ranged over the whole spectrum of Western history, but he was also peculiarly American: he was deeply absorbed in and influenced by the great contemporary social and political issues of his own country, and never more actively so than in the era of Franklin Delano Roosevelt.

The late 1930's were for various writers an open season for shots at the New Deal, as was the Moss Hart and George S. Kaufman satire of President Roosevelt in their musical farce *I'd Rather Be Right* (1937). Anderson was clearly something of a product of his times in following this trend, but the key consideration in understanding his motives is that his great verse plays *Winterset* and *High Tor*, though they brought him money, did not earn enough to suit him; therefore, he wanted to go "commercial" to make still more.[44] In the spring of 1938, he consulted with his neighbor Kurt Weill and then began his first and only musical satire for the professional stage, *Knickerbocker Holiday*, which is for more than one reason considered a minor work. Although the play is technically a collaboration, Anderson, who wrote all of the text himself, used his own ideas for the form and content of the story; he alone wrote the Preface to the published edition;[45] and the Preface hugs closely to the ideology in the story. He reportedly composed the lyrics for the songs in the order in which he came to them in the book, and he sent Weill a nearly complete script ready for the music to be fitted to the words.[46] Following standard practice in The Playwrights' Producing Company, Anderson also sent a draft to his fellow members, whose approval was required for production. They liked it.

From Washington Irving's *A History of New York*, Anderson borrows as his villain the fiercely despotic Peter Stuyvesant, a peg-legged director of New Netherland; and he chooses Irving himself as the author-impresario for this zany, pseudo-historical yarn about a half-Fascist, half-New Deal state whose political difficulties and misadventures in 1647 would cast some light upon conditions in 1938 America. The nominal hero is young Brom Broeck, a Dutch version of Van Dorn, who first gets into trouble by accusing the rascally Mynheer Tienhoven of selling arms and brandy to the Indians, whereupon the state council condemns him to be hanged as a part of the holiday festivities in honor of the governor. Stuyvesant arrives and sets him free, but he soon jails him when he discovers that Broeck is a defiant democrat who suffers from the American's "weakness" of being unable to take orders. Later, Broeck proves himself a hero to the town and persuades the council to re-assert its old powers, clumsy and corrupt though they were, and to reject the arbitrary governor — to keep the government small and amusing so that it will not become oppressive.

When it was first shown, the play appealed to audiences and ran for over five months,[47] a moderate success; however, this record is a pitiful one when it is compared with that of the long-running *Hellzapoppin'* (1938) and with many other shows of Broadway his-

tory. Among the reviewers, J. W. Krutch welcomed the presentation; and Richard Watts, Jr., lauded the acting and singing of Walter
Huston in the role of Stuyvesant, as did the other critics; but he also
judged the comedy to be "ponderous and heavy-handed." And
George Jean Nathan claimed that Anderson knew little about the art
of the musical comedy. Later commentators, save for a very few
such as Mabel Bailey, have not been kind to *Knickerbocker Holiday*;
and it is easy to see why. A successful performance of this work
depends so heavily upon such supporting arts as song, dance, cos-
tuming, and set design that a mere reading of the text may well be
disappointing. Much of the first stage success was due to the earthy,
hilarious portrayal by Walter Huston and also upon Weill's delight-
ful melodies — one of which, "September Song," quickly became a
favorite.[48] The ideas on government would seem old-fashioned
today to many people who believe "big" government is necessary to
counter foreign aggression in the nuclear age, which is one reason
why the play seems never to have been revived.

For understanding Anderson's political ideas as they stood in late
1938, the "Preface to the Politics of *Knickerbocker Holiday*" is
equally valuable as the play itself. In this Preface he does not directly state whether he had meant to satirize any special person or
persons in the New Deal administration, but he leaves no doubt
about his fear that New Deal paternalism was smuggling in the
welfare state under the guise of emergency relief. Like his Brom
Broeck, Anderson warns that paternalism leads finally to absolute
government and the loss of individual liberty. To this playwright,
our corrupt and relatively inefficient democracy in which people are
at least free is preferable to the ruthless but efficient totalitarianism
that in 1938 was steamrolling over various countries of Europe and
Asia.

All along many have agreed that *Knickerbocker Holiday* was intended as a satire on certain excesses and tendencies of the New
Deal. Not only does Anderson in his Preface say so with transparent
indirection, but so does Elmer Rice who calls the play "a not too
subtle attack upon Roosevelt and what Anderson regarded as his
highhanded measures of social reform. The rest of us [in The Playwrights' Producing Company] were strongly pro-Roosevelt, and
though, of course, we had no control over Anderson's script, we did
succeed, mainly by cajolery, in getting him to delete some of the

more pointed references to the New Deal."[49] Stuyvesant correlates handily, if unfairly, with the polio-crippled ex-governor of New York State whose ancestors had settled in the Hudson River Valley when the place was still a Dutch colony. Perhaps the reader will be interested in knowing that President Roosevelt, who had not gone to a play in years, attended this one soon after its opening. The unnamed reporter covering this affair said that the President "laughed heartily at sallies poking fun at the government. . . ." The President and the audience were much amused by a passage in Act II, Scene ii, where Stuyvesant urges his council to make war on Connecticut, at which time the timorous character who is significantly named "Roosevelt" asks whether they could not just as well send them a letter instead — and maybe hand over Boston.[50]

Knickerbocker Holiday terminates Anderson's sound period of creativity — Successful Poetic Dramatist and Political Idealist — which runs from 1930 to 1938. It is, save for the bleak *Golden Six* of his old age, the last time that he belabors government per se, including democracy, as a necessarily corrupting institution; for certain events presaging World War II now made a big change in his art and thought. The first evidence of the change became apparent on the evening of November 20, 1938 (about two weeks after finishing the Preface and during the intermission of a performance of *Knickerbocker Holiday*) when he spoke directly to the theater audience about the recent establishment of many actual Fascist dictatorships. He must have been profoundly concerned inasmuch as he rarely gave public speeches. Along with requesting contributions to a relief fund for German refugees, he cited Nazi Germany in particular for racial and religious persecution that Hitler had begun on November 9–10 with his pogram of the Jews.[51]

In the conclusion to his talk, however, Anderson revealed something new in his political thinking that postdates the composition of the play and maybe the Preface too; for Anderson stated that America might be unable to avoid a war with the dictatorships of Asia and Europe because people might soon learn that the earth could not continue to live half free and half enslaved. Getting into war would mean government restrictions on our own liberties, but Anderson said he was willing to compromise that much for the sake of democracy.[52] He was not merely prophetic but realistic in being willing to put aside for the time his long-nurtured idealism about democracy. And, indeed, World War II did entail many sacrifices of liberty and luxury on the home front.

VIII The Masque of Kings

The theme of rottenness in high places continues in *The Masque of Kings* where Anderson furnishes an answer for the mystery of January 30, 1889, when the young heir to the throne of Austria-Hungary was found with his eighteen-year-old mistress shot to death in a hunting lodge at Mayerling, Austria. In Anderson's version of what happened in that still unsolved affair, the liberal-minded and idealistic Crown Prince Rudolph is so sickened with the killings needed to preserve the regime of his father, Emperor Franz Joseph, that he joins a group of plotters and briefly takes over the throne; but, when he learns that even his beloved Mary Vetsera had formerly been a spy on him for the regime he detests, he gives up the revolution and flees in despair to his hunting lodge. There his Mary joins him and spends the night, their last together; and the next morning, perceiving that he is still shocked at her perfidy, she kills herself in dejection. The Emperor now arrives with pardons for all and even with royal advancement for Rudolph, but the former rebel is unwilling to continue the vapid and futile role of Crown Prince and has no wish to track in the blood of his father's footsteps. Completely frustrated in reaching personal happiness and in accomplishing his political goals of freedom and democracy for the people, the son takes his own cue from the dead Mary and kills himself also. The Emperor hushes up the whole affair — hence, the enigma in recorded history.

One of the recurring motifs in *Winterset*, *Key Largo*, and *The Masque of Kings* is that of Hamlet, the young, idealistic man who is burdened with a great responsibility and who agonizes over his self-doubts and the general worthlessness of the world he is condemned to inhabit. Nevertheless, he wants very much something in which to believe; he finds a doomed love relationship with a sensitive girl; and he finally achieves an inward victory that necessitates or is bound up with his own death. Tempe E. Allison grasped the main weakness of this poetic history drama in remarking that Rudolph has within him sufficient causes of disillusionment and conflict to enable him to rival Prince Hamlet in tragic portraiture, but that Anderson has neglected to arrange these things to represent a person of heroic stature. And so Rudolph "trails off in a weakly sentimental vein instead of in the challenging manner of a great hero."[53]

Allison could have added that the recognition scene (Act II, Scene iii), in which the Prince makes his distressing discoveries, does not actually improve his soul. Granted that by giving up the revolution and killing himself he will thus avoid becoming another murderous emperor, he still seems to have traded one evil for another; and we wonder why, with his newly bestowed authority and with the promise of the Hungarian throne three years hence, he could not peacefully effect at least some of the reforms he advocates; whereas, with him gone, Hungary will continue to suffer as before. It is too bad that Anderson does not give the Emperor or someone else the presence of mind to argue a little in this vein, for the people around Rudolph are oddly inarticulate when he announces the ordinarily alarming topic of suicide. The best his mother can muster is the sentimental notion that she had always wanted to see her son wear the crown someday. Suicide may have been honorable in ancient Rome, and may still be in Japan, but for most of Western civilization today the act smacks of cowardice.

In answer to why Rudolph does not compromise with actuality and try to put his humaneness to work in practical government, Maxwell Anderson would likely argue that, in the context he establishes in the drama, kingship perforce spells bloodshed and injustice, for these are the only means wherewith a ruler can keep himself in power; and that the uncompromising idealist Rudolph, thanks to his father, has no acceptable alternative, not even retirement from the court. As a result of such possible views, it is no wonder that Stark Young considers Act III to be "a suicide pact between the dramatist and the drama."[54] This bias, or this dreadful thesis, that is superimposed on what cries out for a healthful alternative leads us to the conclusion that *The Masque of Kings* is not actually a tragedy but a bleak melodrama whose pathetic hero reminds us of the ineffectual son of Napoleon who dreams of gaining the throne in the poetic *L'Aiglon* by Edmond Rostand. Prince Rudolph shares with Emperor Claudius, covered earlier, a profound sense of the futility of rulership.

Franz Joseph is in some ways a more rounded figure than is his son, and he is certainly just as plausible, if not more so. As a political thinker, he resembles Elizabeth in *Mary of Scotland:* he frankly admits that to him honor, faith, and treason are but words behind which exist the realities of rulership.[55] Although cast as a cynical villain about whom incarnadine deeds are told, his villainy seems too much off-stage and in the past tense for us to dislike him instinctively; except for hamstringing Rudolph's private life, he seems to have no current vices or disfiguring passion or repellent personality quirks; and, consequently, he is not quite the ogre Rudolph leads us to expect. But we are made to believe, however, that he is a dreadfully efficient and an icily vengeful man (yet with a forgiving streak) who can and did put away his wife's lover into some secret dungeon or grave.

As a bold and complex man, Franz Joseph both tyrannizes over and loves his son; and he is even willing to die for him, too, as he proves in Act II, Scene iii, by throwing himself between Rudolph and the assassin Koinoff. In that section of the play, he also indulges his sardonic irony by pointing out, step by irrefutable step, what the revolution must entail if it is to become permanent — that the sensitive Rudolph will soon have to liquidate his own father along with hundreds of other folk, impose censorship, and commit other hateful offenses besides. As Shakespeare put it in *Richard II*, "within the hollow crown / . . . Keeps Death his court" (Act III, Scene ii). Franz Joseph is both impressive and unnerving to us because he knows his son only too well, recognizes how private virtues become imperial weaknesses, and realizes that Rudolph would be like a lamb among the jackals of power politics. Just as the son undergoes development in the play, so does the father; for, after Rudolph has died, Franz Joseph begins to have second thoughts about the pointless role he leads as a sower of death who will in turn be plowed under by a new sower of death, and so on.

Contemporary reviews generally favored the production of *The Masque of Kings* at the Schubert Theatre where it ran for eighty-nine nights after its premiere on February 8, 1937. Stark Young, writing in *The New Republic*, considered the play entertaining up to the final act, where Rudolph then "goes off into a sheer licking of lyric chops" — which is Young's response to the rhetoric-not-quite-turned-poetry which mars many passages. In the *New York Times*, Brooks Atkinson called the work "a searching study of character. . . ." But the unsigned writer in *Literary Digest*, while praising the "fine flights of eloquence," complained of Anderson's "addiction to a theme of futility" that was becoming clearer play by play. One of the most glittering reviews came from J. W. Krutch, of *The Nation*, who employed such phrases as "Theatrically . . . extraordinarily effective," "thoroughly mastered the grand romantic manner," and "the best of Mr. Anderson's plays [since *Winterset*]." Later commentators have for the most part been far cooler in their appraisal, partly owing, I believe, to the likelihood that they have never seen a staging of the work — revivals seem to be scarce or nonexistent. Jordan Y. Miller, by some perversity of taste, seems to prefer *The Masque of Kings* above *Valley Forge* and all the Tudor plays put together.[56] I am convinced that we are dealing here with one of the more interesting but lesser products of Maxwell Anderson; I say this, too, though cognizant that the play is one of a handful of his to fare well abroad.[57]

Perhaps it will interest some readers to learn that the real Countess Larisch, mentioned in the first edition, sued Anderson for libel. He had had no idea that she was still alive. Judiciously he withdrew the first printing and substituted the name Baronin von Neustadt, which meant a change in her husband's name as well.[58]

IX   Both Your Houses

As we can see in the next play, constitutional government in America, just a few decades later, is less dangerous to human life but still another example of the corruption of power. *Both Your Houses* (note the Shakespearean echo) exists in two complete versions — the 1933 published one which we shall look at first, and the 1939 unpublished one. These two versions illustrate Anderson's changing attitude toward democracy and the possibilities of individual fulfillment. Barrett Clark and George Freedley praise *Both Your Houses* as "the first play of any moment written by an American that dealt exclusively or largely with political crookedness in the federal government"[59]; but its main predecessor seems to have been Harrison G. Rhodes and Thomas A. Wise's *A Gentleman from Mississippi* (1908) which was also concerned with the loading of a Congressional appropriation bill with graft.[60]

Both Your Houses reached the stage of the Royale Theatre on March 6, 1933; but, if it had arrived when Anderson first wanted it to and if a producer had not kept delaying its presentation until the Hoover administration, the original target of the satire, was out of office,[61] the point would have been sharper and the stage run perhaps longer than one hundred and twenty nights. There is the consolation, however, that the Pulitzer Prize committee recognized with its award for the 1932–33 season that the work had certain values which were presumably not completely dependent upon "timeliness." However belated in its production, the play was not altogether useless as social criticism: it made a valuable appeal to the new federal administration, containing one hundred and twenty-seven new members, that was readying to assemble in Washington at the crisis of the Depression and correct the wrongs of the Hoover era. But whether any such politicians attended or read the play is a matter about which I have no information.

The narrative illustrates once more Anderson's stance of despair. An idealistic freshman congressman, Alan McClean, whose surname is an apt characteronym for his sterling makeup, learns that an omnibus House appropriation bill is laden with "pork barrel" as well as graft which will cost the already over-taxed public many millions of dollars. One of the congressmen, Sol Fitzmaurice, has even tagged on a measure that will anchor the Atlantic fleet off his private resort area rather than Hampton Roads. Alan opposes the bill despite its inclusion of funds for a dam project in his own district, for he has recently learned about the dishonest bidding for the contract, a bidding engineered by his backer and campaign manager.

Meanwhile, most of McClean's fellow congressmen have no scruples whatever in using skulduggery; in fact, dishonesty is so routine that they are surprised that Alan raises any objections. Sol, a somehow likeable old rascal and the most individualized figure in the play, candidly asserts that the processes of government absolutely depend upon graft and that this very nation was built by brigands who looted the treasury and the national resources. In Alan's research about the tainted appropriation bill, he encounters a moral dilemma: he learns that the committee chairman, Gray, an essentially honest man and the father of the girl he is courting, has innocently compromised himself by owning stock in an insolvent bank which the money in the bill would probably save. But Alan chooses to follow his conscience and try to defeat the bill, even at the risk of ruining the man he admires. Unable to block the legislation in committee, he loads onto it such flagrantly colossal riders that the whole thing will, he hopes, fail when it comes to a vote in Congress. Astonishingly, it passes anyway.[62]

Of the various technical excellences in Anderson's construction of this play, a critic would have to concede the advantage of subordinating the love relationship to the drama of ideas: at the end, there is no forced or sentimental reconciliation between Alan and Marjorie, at least on stage; indeed, no more than two lines are devoted to the whole business. Moreover, Alan is also not portrayed as a knight in shining armor (he exposes his own campaign), otherwise he would differentiate the forces of good and evil either too neatly or too obviously. Still, he is clearly and believably a heroic figure, even though, like many of the Shaw and the Ibsen male creations, he lacks well-roundedness. John H. Lawson has sharply criticized the conception of McClean because he is not made to ask himself, " 'How can I live and achieve integrity under these conditions [?]' "; because he has no rational solution for the dilemma of government in which he finds himself; because he admittedly has no conviction as to what the best type of government is; because, therefore, he has no specific proposal for reform; and because "the very condition against which McClean is fighting is brought about by the apathy or uncertainty of people as to 'the best kind of government.' "[63]

In countering Lawson's first point, I contend that McClean has had, at least for the time being, his bridges burned behind him: if he stayed in, as Lawson seems to suggest, and publicly denounced his colleagues as dishonest, this legislator who had won his office under a cloud of suspicion would cut a sorry figure! But, it seems to me that Alan McClean might become more successful at winning sympathy and support for his exposure of the others as the voluntarily resigned congressman that Anderson plans him to be — providing he could write a book or afford a lecture tour. As the novice legislator that we find him to be at the end of the story, he realizes that he has already cost the country a vast amount of unnecessary money in trying to outwit the crooks; for him, then, it seems wise to choose a field of combat in which the public will not have to pay through the nose for his inexperience.

As for McClean's supposed fault of not having any rational solution to the dilemma of government, I believe that Lawson is simply unfair in asking such a newcomer, already a disastrous failure in politics, to have figured out on short notice what has eluded for centuries the most eminent philosophers, social scientists, and statesmen. Anyway, no playwright is or should be required to offer a solution to the social problems he presents; it is quite enough to lay forth the problem in an entertaining manner. Apropos Lawson's last objection, the hero in this play does *not*, I maintain, act apathetically or uncertainly about what he wants done, which is clearly a public exposure leading to reform. It would be grossly unfair to equate Alan McClean's patriotic state of mind with that of the general electorate who tolerate Sol Fitzmaurice and his hoggish breed. At worst, McClean is an idealist who is unwilling to accommodate himself to working out in the hurly-burly of "dirty politics" the kinds of rewards that Congressman Gray finds and is satisfied with.

Though mainly a drama of ideas in which there is scant physical action, the narrative nevertheless grips the attention from the moment Alan enters in Act I to his angry exit in Act III. Unquestionably, the amusing secondary characters go far to sustain this interest; and these include Alan's fast-talking but honest secretary, Bus, and the eloquent old tippler and jovial antagonist, Sol Fitzmaurice. The dialogue is crisp throughout, and Maxwell Anderson illustrates in this dialogue his special and much-overlooked gift for lifelike vernacular in plays with contemporary settings.

Both Your Houses (1933), notwithstanding its gloom, is a shade lighter on the scale of optimism than is typical of Anderson's plays of the 1930's wherein the ideal is impossible of attainment in social institutions and human affairs.[64] The pessimism of this published version was, incidentally, still more intense in the three preliminary drafts that now survive. These drafts start near the close of Act II to emphasize McClean's moral struggle about whether to save Gray or to remain true to the national interest; but the published version emphasizes throughout the external struggle between McClean and the sponsors of the bill. In the early drafts, McClean is unable to stay true to the national interest because, upon learning of Gray's predicament with the bank, he is so conscience-stricken about the possibility of ruining the honest Gray that he decides to endorse the bill to protect this man even at the loss of his own professional ideals. At the end, after McClean's realization that the prestigious United States House of Representatives does not by any latitude of thinking embrace the good of the nation, he resigns his post to return to teaching. The upshot is that, as an idealist trying to make the actual world over into his own image, he had no choice but to fail one way or the other.

Consequently, the preparatory drafts of *Both Your Houses* are stained with that very spirit of hopelessness which permeates other early Anderson dramaturgy. But late in rehearsals significant changes were introduced — most likely at the suggestion of other theater people engaged in the production — which sharpened the satirical point considerably. These changes allowed at least the possibility of public altruism and constructive reform despite the consuming self-interest that allegedly motivates leaders in government. As such, the published version of *Both Your Houses* is evidently a compromise, scarcely to be regretted on our part, between what Anderson felt in his heart about government and what the production staff felt was expedient in order to secure a viable drama.

Fortunately, however, the slightly revised *Both Your Houses* that Anderson prepared for a staging at the Pasadena Community Playhouse, Pasadena, California, during July of 1939, has never seen print. The new writing consists of two new speeches for McClean that are, sad to relate, inconsistent with the tone of what had gone before; but they do reflect the author's latest convictions at that time to defend democracy from the threat that Hitler's Germany was making to the free peoples of the earth. And so, after staring at the totalitarianism that was spreading like cancer over the body of Europe, Anderson now viewed our imperfect democracy as a relatively healthy system that was well worth saving.[65]

The development of Anderson's thinking — as illustrated by the early plays up through most of the 1930's — was from a posture of idealism that could not be satisfied in the actual world where self-interest is always rearing its ugly head to a posture of practical accommodation with the actual when the threat of World War II made him take a second look, a fond one this time, at the values of democracy. *Candle in the Wind*, *The Eve of St. Mark*, *Storm Operation*, and even *Journey to Jerusalem* (which is not covered in this book) all reveal the patriot Anderson who is laboring in the service of the actual. Avery tells us that there are even some unpublished comedies composed during the 1950's — "Adam, Lilith and Eve" and "Madonna and Child" — which ridicule those persons who try to win to the ideal.[66]

CHAPTER 4

From *"Sea-Wife"* to Bad Seed

THE plays discussed in this chapter constitute a broad miscellany which in itself indicates the resistance of Anderson's varied drama to classification; yet, they all happen to deal with American citizens or immigrants of the nineteenth and twentieth centuries who are beset with one or more problems such as legal injustice, tragic love, commercial greed, chronic dissatisfaction with job and marriage, racial and religious intolerance, and bad heredity. For the most part, these plays are even more relevant than the previously discussed ones to contemporary problems of the "little" man, the private citizen, who has nothing to do with playing a role in the battlefield, in the palace, or in the elected assembly. Most of the plays embody poetry or fantasy or both.

I *"Sea-Wife"*

Of Anderson's two verse plays that treat with nineteenth-century New England, "Sea-Wife" and *The Wingless Victory*, the former is by far less known. A singular piece written in 1924, "Sea-Wife" has neither been published nor professionally staged.[1] A thing of "strange and peculiar beauty" is how Barrett Clark described this poetic fantasy, a copy of which the playwright had sent him along with word that it contained some poetry that Anderson liked.[2] Because "Sea-Wife" is so much superior to some of the Anderson plays that did get to Broadway and because it has distinct literary merit, this work merits our attention.

The acknowledged source of "Sea-Wife" is Matthew Arnold's poem "The Forsaken Merman" in which a sea king mourns for his human wife who has deserted him and has returned to live among her race. Anderson uses a remote island off the coast of Maine as the setting for his romance. Unlike Arnold, he shifts the burden of tragic

101

feeling to the wife, Margaret, who, as the play begins, has just returned after a mysterious three-year absence to her fisherman husband, Dan, so that, as she explains, she can enjoy once more the warmth of human affection and also save her soul. She tells Dan that the cruel merman had granted her only three days ashore and that she has already used nine days; and nightly, in sounds inaudible to other mortals, she hears her lonely sea mate with their children calling to her from the waves.

Dan, however, refuses to believe there is a sea king; and the only person in the tiny community who confirms the reality of Margaret's "dream," as she now terms it, is a witch, a doubtful informant. And so Margaret's conflict — whether it lies in a mind insane or under enchantment, or whether in the dilemma of inhabiting two worlds of being (cf. *High Tor*) — consists in her deciding whether to stay with her mortal husband or to go back to the children she longs for. The author conveys well the longing, heartbreak, and *aloneness* of a woman who is torn between two equally demanding and excluding allegiances and who is hemmed in, meanwhile, by superstitious and heartless neighbors. When a fisherman reports that he has seen the bodies of two dead children lying on the beach, the dead children are proof to Margaret that the sea king has taken vengeance on her little ones. Margaret now wishes for death, feeling that she has betrayed her family. Later, the neighbors find her body, dead by mysterious means.

The poetry in "Sea-Wife," though it does not reach the heights of *High Tor* or *Winterset*, goes beyond the polished-prose-and-rhetoric of which so much Anderson verse drama consists and is quite attractive in places. Here is an excerpt from one of the speeches of Dr. Fallon, a preacher on the island, as he describes man's mortality amid the boundless isolation of the cosmos:

> . . . Island and sea adhere
> To a dark star adrift about a flame,
> And the flame falls forever through a night
> Unknown, forever unknown.
> Those of us who are old
> Know we live briefly as a light on water,
> Passing and gone.
> . . . .
> Our lips and hands are a little

Shaken dust that has slept before we came
And will sleep sound again.

from Act II

There are tragic overtones in "Sea-Wife," though the work is not a tragedy in the usual sense of the word. Because this play is not adaptable to the commercial tastes of Broadway, save under the most exceptional sensitivity of acting and directing, it deserves a place in the repertoire of the "little theater."

II   The Wingless Victory

Like the foregoing play, *The Wingless Victory* (1936) is decidedly Romantic, uses a New England seaside locale, explores the motif of intolerance and bigotry, has for its main figure a woman whose children are born under a strange marriage and die from parental betrayal, is written partly in verse, and has as its basis of inspiration a famous work of earlier literature. In the present case, the inspiration comes from Euripides's *Medea;* and, though having numerous points of difference, *Medea* and *The Wingless Victory* share in common the exotic account of an adventurous man who brings back from a long and dangerous voyage a barbarian princess for his wife; he soon deserts her; afterwards, the woman kills her two children.

Nathaniel McQuestion, after having left Salem many years earlier as a vagabond sailor who was determined never to return home until he was rich enough to "buy" the town, sails back in 1800 on the *Queen of the Celebes* with a cargo of spices; and he arrives just in time to bolster the fortunes of his needy family. He brings, also, into the narrow-minded, Puritanical community not only a beautiful Malayan princess, Oparre, as his wife but also their two dusky children. Neither his mother's family nor the town at large can stomach this miscegenation, even though the noble Oparre is a converted Christian; but they do not scruple to accept his lavish loans and investments. McQuestion, foolishly believing that he can buy the town's good will, fails to obtain a single social invitation. As soon as they have milked him of most of his fortune, a group of Salemites confront him with their knowledge that his ship is actually a stolen vessel formerly called *The Wingless Victory;* and they coerce him into getting rid of his wife and children as the price for his safety and solvency. By this time, McQuestion has absorbed so effectively the values of the detested community that he reluctantly accedes to their wishes by choosing materialism over the woman who loves him. Again aboard ship, Oparre poisons herself and her children out of despair because they now have no place of refuge — not even Malaya, where her father would kill her. McQuestion at last suffers a change of heart and goes to her repentant, but he is too late.

The Wingless Victory ran for one hundred and ten performances during its first stage enactment, and the illustrious Katharine Cornell played the role of Oparre. Nonetheless, reviewers and later commentators have examined this work with undisguised disappointment and have exposed its major faults. If McQuestion was intended to be a tragic hero, as seems to have been the case, then the play fails artistically because of his depiction. Mabel Bailey probably wrote the definitive pronouncement on this subject by asserting that McQuestion is a pathetic rather than a tragic figure: he returned home intending to flaunt his riches and "torment his pious Puritan family by bringing a dark-skinned wife into their smug little New England town"; but, since his method of acquiring money has been by piracy, which has not equipped him to manage such money, he easily falls prey to the sharp citizens. Moreover, his motives are hardly better than those of the townsmen he deprecates because he is equally "dependent on money and its prestige as the Puritans he despises, and dependent, too, on their acceptance of him." After he has been outwitted by his brother, McQuestion "collapses at once," having "no resources of knowledge or wisdom or fortitude for making a place [anywhere] for himself and his wife. . . ."[3]

On the other hand, Miss Bailey praises Oparre as one of Anderson's finest creations, an evaluation which, in the light of most of the serious, published criticism on this play, seems at best wishful. I have to agree with Joseph Wood Krutch who observes that Oparre is not at all convincing as a person: "she seems a vague blend of the genuinely primitive with some sort of ideal humanity," is "never any more than an abstraction modeled in wax," and does not possess enough "character of her own to engage our emotions."[4] Krutch's evaluation is based mainly, if not solely, upon the theater performance; but the evaluation seems to me sound now even after a third reading of the text. Indeed, distressingly few individualizing details serve to mark Oparre as a particular human being rather than as the embodiment of a myth. Arthur Sampley, who is one of several critics to argue in this wise, notes that Oparre "breathes something of the air of unreality which pervades this play."[5] Still, of the two major characters, Oparre is much the more sensitively conceived, and the better poetry always comes from her lips alone, as in Act III, Scene ii, where she cradles her daughter Durian on her knee and marvels at the beauty of this dying, unwanted child. The third act is, of course, sheer melodrama.

III   Gods of the Lightning

Social injustice figures also in the next play to be discussed, *Gods of the Lightning* (1928). Some facts about the Sacco-Vanzetti case that made headlines around the world relate to both this play and to *Winterset* (1935). Following the murder of a paymaster and guard on April 15, 1920, the two poor Italian aliens named Nicola Sacco and Bartolomeo Vanzetti were arrested and brought to trial before the Massachusetts Superior Court. Since the two defendants were avowed Anarchists who had alledgedly evaded the draft, these factors evidently weighed heavily with the jury despite the pleas of innocence and the circumstantiality of the incriminating evidence. Antiradical feeling ran high in the United States at the time because of the recent Bolshevik revolution in Russia and because of the activities of the International Woodsmen of the World and other groups in the United States. The jury found the two aliens guilty, whereupon radicals and Socialists immediately protested the men's innocence and claimed — what is widely believed by many thoughtful people today — that they had been convicted mainly for their revolutionary, Anarchistic beliefs. Despite the fact that a condemned criminal, one Celestino Madeiros, confessed that he had participated in the crime and that the Sacco-Vanzetti pair were innocent, they were not benefitted.

When the immigrants were sentenced to death, such a hurricane of protest swept the nation that the governor of Massachusetts appointed an independent investigating committee to review the trial proceedings, a committee that included a former judge, Robert Grant (note the Judge Gaunt in *Winterset*). The governor refused clemency, the reviewing committee agreed with his position, and Sacco and Vanzetti were executed in August of 1927. The whole affair has ever since been the subject of intense controversy in and out of books, including numerous works of literature; yet, just a year after the execution, the Chief of the Licensing Division of the City of Boston, J.M. Case, ruled that Maxwell Anderson and Harold Hickerson's *Gods of the Lightning* was practically "anarchistic and treasonable" and should not, therefore, be licensed for presentation in that city.[6]

In *Gods of the Lightning,* Vanzetti becomes Dante Capraro, the gentle and humane Anarchist; Sacco is greatly transformed into the native-born American James Macready, a militant International Woodsmen of the World leader; and Madeiros is changed into the bleak-minded and fatalistic restaurant owner Suvorin. As the three-act play opens, a henchman employed by Suvorin has botched a robbery by killing the paymaster. Elsewhere in the "city on the eastern seaboard," Macready and Capraro, who are unaware of the killing, are occupied with strike business when they are arrested and "framed" by the police for the crime. While on the witness stand, each of the innocent men levels indictments against the corruption of the capitalist society. In the legal system used against them, we see incredible abuses: the foreman of the jury, who is bent on liquidating all "red" agitators, even stands up in the jury box to assail Macready for an alleged bombing attack; the snaky district attorney blackmails witnesses to obtain false testimony; the biased and stupid judge issues unfair rulings to help the prosecution. When Suvorin proves the pair's innocence by confessing his own guilt, the court will not admit his testimony because he has a previous criminal record. The jury turns in a verdict of guilty; Macready and Capraro must die; and, in the final scene, the friends of the condemned men wait in vain for the governor's pardon while the clock ticks off the fatal minutes.[7]

In this extremely topical social tract, ideas are paramount, not characterization. Macready is not conceived along heroic lines; and the reader only feels sorry for him. Capraro fares no better. Rosalie, who is Macready's fiancee, is just a girl who, tenderhearted about violence, does not want to see the radicals go to jail or be executed. The villains, with the exception of Suvorin, are so unrelievably evil as to make us doubt their basic humanity. In other words, Anderson and Hickerson shunt aside the complexities of human behavior to give us an indignantly one-sided and propagandistic account of social injustice that is practically devoid of literary interest. Although Anita Block praises *Gods of the Lightning* for its left-wing message,[8] practically all serious commentators rightly dismiss the work on some valid count or other; and they most commonly do so as a brand of journalism that is too forced for lasting appeal or too distorted to be of historical interest.

IV Winterset

Winterset, likewise inspired by the Sacco-Vanzetti affair, is markedly better as pure literature, for the passage of years helped Maxwell Anderson to attain a needed esthetic distance. With *Winterset*, he seems to have realized that he was giving theater audiences one of the most startling and original dramas yet to emerge from his little cabin in the woods[9] and that it was startling but not wholly in the sensational manner of *Gods of the Lightning*. The play is also significant for its several "firsts": it was the first time that anyone had seriously tried on the professional stage a poetic tragedy with a *contemporary* setting; and it won for its author the first Drama Critics Circle Award ever given.[10]

In the summer of 1933, while at work on *Mary of Scotland*, Anderson began to contemplate writing a modern tragedy in verse; for this innovation would, he felt, help offset the undesired reputation of "historical playwright" which *Mary of Scotland* would confirm. His deep conviction, as stated earlier in this book, held that today's tragedies could and should be wrought in verse; but, in projecting such an innovative work for himself, he found it difficult to find an "idiom" acceptable to audiences. He reasoned that poetry in a modern, upper-class setting would have to entail stylization that might well detract from the realism he felt was necessary; and, on the other hand, he wanted to avoid the "far away" equally as much as he did the "long ago" and yet retain an element of strangeness. As a result of his objectives, he compromised.[11]

His setting for *Winterset* is a slum neighborhood that squats at the base of a gigantic bridgehead of masonry and steel whose enormous span arcs over the heads of the audience, and his characters' speech is free of modern clichés. His characters compose an uncommon gathering during a December thunderstorm, for they include an insane ex-judge, an impassioned and inspired young wanderer, a dying killer, and various slum denizens. This tremendous bridge setting — symbolic of the contiguity of wealth and poverty, of inhuman power and defenseless little folk below, and yet of the aspir-

ing hopes of all mankind — is in Anderson's art approached only by
the steam shovel in *High Tor*. In fact, the title of this new composition, the writing of which took place between March 21 and June 1,
1935, was "The Bridge."[12] The final choice of title, *Winterset*, is
explained in one of Mio's loveliest speeches in Act III where he
refers to the winter solstice of December 21–22.[13]

The plot, ordinarily suited to literary Naturalism, concerns
doomed young love that defeats the desire for revenge in a social
order that discriminates against a disadvantaged group and benefits
one class at the expense of another. Thirteen years before the story
in the play begins, an Italian-American radical named Romagna was
"framed" for a murder committed by the gangster Trock Estrella,
who subsequently went to prison on another charge. After Romagna's execution, his son Mio, who suffered from prejudice in his
home town, began to wander about America in search of evidence
that would vindicate his father. When the curtain rises, Mio, ac-
companied by his friend Carr, visits a tenement near the Manhattan
waterfront because he learned that somewhere in the neighborhood
dwelt a man who knew that Romagna was innocent, and there he
meets and falls in love with fifteen-year-old Miriamne, the daughter
to a kindly and philosophical old rabbi. Her brother is none other
than Garth Esdras, a former henchman for Trock and the material
witness to the murder; but Garth had never testified at the trial.
However, Trock, now fresh out of prison and wary that new evidence might re-open the Romagna case, frightens Garth into silence
and seclusion; Miriamne later questions her brother about this visitor and is alarmed to learn of her brother's complicity. Old Esdras
tries to comfort Miriamne with his brand of fatalistic, sophistical
reasoning by saying that she is alarmed only because of her innocent
youth. Also converging on the scene is the formerly presiding judge
at the Romagna trial, Gaunt, now mad, who has been blaming himself for his prejudicial role in the trial; he is seeking out Garth to
learn whether the new rumored evidence would have made any
difference in the verdict. Gaunt begins to rave, whereupon Trock
orders his cohort Shadow to kill him; but, when Shadow refuses, the
latter is killed at Trock's orders and thrown into the river, which
brings Act I to its conclusion.

In Act II, Gaunt and Mio meet at Esdras' cellar apartment; Garth
denies he has any evidence on the Romagna murder; and, to make
matters worse for Mio, the self-tortured Gaunt almost convinces

him that the boy's father was actually guilty. Gaunt's argument and Mio's growing doubts help make *Winterset* the most complex psychological drama of all of Anderson's works. The boy's plight grows desperate when he learns that his sweetheart's own brother is the one who is withholding the crucial information, but he soon gets the information anyway in a rather strange episode which happens when Trock, who is returning to abduct the ex-judge while a Lear-like thunderstorm rages outside, is startled to see Shadow stagger in from the river covered with blood and seeking revenge. Trock thereby thinks he sees a ghost; and, thus frightened, he blurts out during a mock trial held by Gaunt the news that Romagna was entirely innocent. The turning point in the drama draws near when some policemen enter on a search. Mio, yearning to report to them the murder of Shadow who was taken dying into the next room, goes unbelieved because he had earlier taunted a policeman outside; then, waxing insistent, he is checked just in time by Miriamne, who wants to protect her brother. "You have dreamed something — isn't it true?" she pleads (Act II). Comprehending her ruse, he agrees — for now he is too much enamored of her to do otherwise — but it is precisely by such forbearance that he unwittingly prepares for his own death. Trock will now arrange to silence him forever.

The third and final act returns Carr to the neighborhood ready to help his friend who, this time, out of discretion, plays an uncommunicative Hamlet to his friend's Horatio. But, by keeping silent for the sake of his sweetheart's brother, by sending Carr away uninformed, Mio loses his last chance for safety. Mio explains to the girl that, out of consideration for her, he has lost his desire for revenge; and he tells her that he now looks forward to a better life — to one filled with hope, instead of fear — although he cannot yet forgive those who brought his father to execution. To Miriamne, he pleads, "But teach me how to live and forget to hate!" (Act III). With this situation and these words the recognition scene commences; and it is complete when this gentle, intelligent girl of the slums convinces him that Mio's father, were he alive, would assuredly forgive his enemies. She teaches him that he does not have to prove his father's innocence to the world, for he has already wrung from Garth the truth of that innocence. Just before Mio leaves her to flee the neighborhood, he exults, "I came here seeking / light in darkness, / running from the dawn, / and stumbled on a morning."[14] These lines are not only richly poetic and meaningful in themselves but also bitterly ironic. After making a ghastly allusion to Persephone — one of the various foreshadowings of his death — he goes outside where the waiting thugs shoot him down. Now defiant with hopeless grief, Miriamne also invites their bullets; for, like the Juliet in another star-crossed drama, she cannot bear to survive without her beloved.

Several reviewers of the early performances of *Winterset* felt compelled to attend this astonishing play twice; some read the text before writing the second notices; and some thoughtful second notices made the play a triumph at the box office.[15] This novel experiment in drama does require careful examination to disclose not merely all its qualities but the rationale behind some details that might otherwise seem troublesome and unrealistic. Mio's characterization, for one, has drawn some unnecessarily adverse commentary that is primarily about his educational sophistication; and other characters, such as Gaunt and Esdras, have too often been misunderstood by critics of this play.

About seventeen, Mio is the son of a radical who, we may conjecture, was surely a reader and probably headed a reading family. Mio has had schooling through part of the secondary level, including a stay at Hollywood High School which he apparently attended strictly on his own initiative because, at that time, he had no guardian to advise or care for him; and he was forced (note!) to leave this school for lack of a permanent address. Such a drive for learning suggests intellectual curiosity and a maturity beyond his years. Among the various possible places in which to keep warm in Manhattan, he chose to spend the winter in the public library, and once there he must have felt constrained, sooner or later, to read books in order to pass muster with the watchful librarians if not to avoid an otherwise inescapable boredom. And he actually does attribute his education — perhaps exaggerating somewhat — to this experience. A winter is probably longer than the time most college students in the United States spend in the library during their entire four years of education.

Somewhere along the way, Mio became acquainted with French poetry and with the writings of Sigmund Freud, Christopher Marlowe, Alfred, Lord Tennyson (part of the "driven snow of Victorian literature" that Mio is proud of having explored), and no doubt with the material of other literary figures who are not within the ken of most high school students. His kind of knowledge and his bookish experience are rare but still credible in an intelligent person with so unusual a background, despite what Block and Bailey contend.[16] Additionally, Mio is clearly one whose senses and perceptions have been sharpened, like those of Robert Browning's young Fra Lippo Lippi, through his early exposure in the streets and alleys where he had to thrive as best he could on the crusts of strangers. And had not Maxwell Anderson endowed him thus with a multifold awareness, well suited to the Romantic hero, we would not be so ready to accept from Mio the finest flights of poetry in all the dialogue.

This factor brings us, however, to the objection sometimes heard that we cannot plausibly expect Mio, Miriamne, and the gangsters to speak in poetry. In answer, I should say first that the play is by design only partly realistic; the reader or theatergoer must perforce suspend *some* of his disbelief. Moreover, Shakespeare's Romeo and Juliet spoke to each other in poetry, even composed a sonnet together — at tenderer ages than those of their counterparts in *Winterset* — and audiences today cheerfully and gratefully accept this precedent. As for the hoodlums, no one who reads or hears their dialogue need be troubled, however, by any sense of incongruity or by the belief that poetry is squandered on them. A careful check of *Winterset* shows that the underworld figures receive comparatively unpoetic lines; actually, theirs is a flat although somewhat rhythmical prose that happens to be arranged to look like verse.

Joseph Wood Krutch's response to objections about the speech of the gangsters seems to me relevant and decisive: "[T]he appropriateness or inappropriateness of elevated speech depends (as Shakespeare will sufficiently demonstrate) not upon the speaker's social or even intellectual status but upon the success of his creator in endowing him with an intensity of feeling for the expression of which the best utterance is none too good. . . ."[17] Anderson's intermixing of formal poetic utterance with a good measure of realism in character and situation is enough to severely challenge the accepted literary tradition; nonetheless, despite the advertising for the first stage presentation that openly admitted that the work was in poetry, this frankness did not deter crowds from attending. The fame of *Winterset* now testifies that millions have learned to accept, perhaps welcome, with some degree of pleasure Anderson's once radical experiment in poetic dialogue.

On the other hand, the dramatic poetry is not always more successful in this play than it is in most of the other leading verse dramas by Anderson; for its does not *invariably* lift the spirit, evoke the rapture of true love, or delight with dazzling images. As poetry, the iambic verse is as much reflective and meditative as it is lyrical. Mio's report about going fishing for mackerel in the beautiful Pacific is one of several instances where the versified language rings ungenuine, contrived, and flat (Act I, Scene iii). Occasionally, the emotion becomes as distanced and as subtly condescending as it does when Mio tells his inamorata to go and resume her small domestic duties; indeed, this last passage sounds more like Anderson than Mio. Rarely does the playwright give Miriamne anything in the way of heightened language comparable to the purple flights of her beloved, but his excuse may be that she is less educated and because she functions largely as an audience for Mio and as his passive love object. But we must admit that successfully balanced love duets in poetic form are uncommon in dramatic history and that most examples that appear do so in the works of such masters as Shakespeare and William Congreve (*The Way of the World*).

In regard to Gaunt and Esdras, both of whom have been misunderstood in some of the published criticism, Gaunt is one of the most fully realized characters in all of Anderson's plays. He is a little unusual for a former judge in being himself a victim of the class injustice which he in his own time helped perpetrate. Unlike the one-dimensional judge in *Gods of the Lightning*, this man is truly complex and therefore elicits from us mixed feelings, among which we find pity because he has only once, in an otherwise unstained career (if we can believe him), been accused of a miscarriage of justice. Gaunt sincerely agonizes over that one unforgettable error, but there is no atonement or solace for him in sight, not even in the Hebraic "wisdom" of Esdras.[18] His confessed fallibility serves to help Mio relent in his passionate search for revenge. In a letter, Gertrude Anderson wrote that her husband actually built *Winterset* around a real ex-judge; furthermore, she declared that Gaunt is in no sense an invention or a derivation from Shakespeare (critics who think he originated in Lear are therefore mistaken) but that he is based on an actual person who was deranged in the very way presented in the drama.[19]

Esdras' role is equally interesting, yet he is often either ignored or misinterpreted in what has seen print. Esdras goes to some length to convince his son Garth, of whom he is naturally solicitous, to keep silent about his guilt because a confession will lead only to more suffering, and because, he says, no true justice is possible in this imperfect world. But Garth has somehow learned independently, like the lovers, to expect and demand justice in this world; and thus the father's otherworldly vision and resignation have made no impress at all on the children. Later, at the opening of Act II, Esdras advises Miriamne that his wisdom is useless except for old people. Even his long studies in the Talmud have not given him hard and certain answers. Therefore, in the context of the play he clearly has next to no advice that these young people will accept, committed as they are to the ideal of individual responsibility in this life for wrongs done. His sorrow and fear for his son do not allow him to be quite objective either. His role is like that of a foolish old Polonius who is full of subtle religious saws that are unfit for modern stratagems. I much doubt, despite what Samuel Kliger argues, that Esdras has any significant effect in causing Mio to renounce his desire for revenge.[20] Miriamne is far more instrumental in this way.

Maxwell Anderson, I contend, is not offering Esdras' brand of "wisdom" for anyone's approval. Gloomy as Anderson was about the possibility of realizing justice in human society, he continued to pursue the ideal. As evidence, he offers in an essay from this very period what appears to be an explicit judgment of the Esdras-type; there he states that people who have surrendered their belief in justice and truth and who no longer strive for them are traitors to themselves and to the race![21] Far from being the teacher, Esdras shows in his peroration over the bodies of the dead young lovers that it is *he* who has learned a lesson from them: they exemplify a glory possible to man, namely the willingness, for the sake of love, to face certain defeat and even death with bravery and defiance.

Winterset is the result of Anderson's application of his rules of tragedy, as are some of the history plays; but whether *Winterset* is a tragedy or a serious melodrama is in much dispute. The play contains all the essential ingredients of tragedy *if* a figure from humble life is allowed to be the hero — and he is, evidently, in this age when Aristotle is no longer the sole guide in dramaturgy. Anderson's liberal use of melodrama, especially that connected with the gangsters, is doubtless the biggest single feature that makes some people hesitate to class the work as tragedy. It must be remembered, however, that many of Shakespeare's tragedies contain melodramatic elements also. Incidentally, the first motion picture version (1936) transformed the tragic story into a melodrama by shifting the emphasis from character, where it belongs, to situation. Quite late in the film a serious deviation from Anderson's text occurs: Mio and Miriamne find a secret route past the gangsters and out of the neighborhood so that they can enjoy a life free of class distinction and miscarried justice.[22] But this slick transformation defies the carefully laid groundwork of foreshadowings and character-initiated action in Anderson's original script that gives his ending its inevitability.

The influence of Shakespeare upon the text is not hard to find. As the would-be avenger of his father's death who veers from his vengeance because of his concern for nice distinctions, who learns from a play-within-a-play the truth he is seeking, and who dies in his youth struck down by his enemies, Mio clearly reminds readers of Hamlet. But the influence is probably broader than that of Shakespeare; for, as Francis E. Abernethy has observed, *Winterset* has "every characteristic of the classical revenge tragedy except the revenge conclusion."[23] Notwithstanding Gertrude Anderson's claim concerning the origin of Gaunt, this man's insane singing of dirty songs has a certain Ophelia ring about it; moreover, the hobo who appears in the mock trial enacts Mad Tom 'o Bedlam to Gaunt's Lear. As in *Macbeth*, an accusing ghost (Shadow) is employed to frighten someone into signs of guilt. Possibly the most noticeable resemblance is to *Romeo and Juliet*: two innocent young people meet for the first time at a dance, they fall in love without at first realizing that a barrier interposes between their families, and a holy man advises and warns them — to no avail.

V   High Tor

Like *Winterset*, the locale for *High Tor* is also New York State and the time setting is the present. The reader might be curious about the actual mountain High Tor that figures in the play by that name and whose features, inhabitants, and traditions are inextricably bound up with that amazing work. From the attic of Anderson's old farmhouse, the visitor can descry, about three miles distant, the part of South Mountain occupied by this famous landmark. It towers on the west bank of the Hudson River, alongside the expanse known as the Tappan Zee which was made famous long ago in the charming stories of Washington Irving; and it overlooks the village of Haverstraw. About eight hundred and thirty-two feet high, the summit bears a steel tower on which stands the airplane beacon mentioned in the play; from the summit, the visitor can see miles of exhilarating scenery up and down the river. Found all over the wooded slopes of High Tor during the 1930's were wild mountain laurel, blueberries, poison ivy, and plenty of copperheads and rattlers; today, the slopes bear a vineyard.

This eminence at the north end of the Palisades of the Hudson — about forty miles north of New York City — is the subject of various legends, such as the one that the Three Wise Men built there an altar to the infant Christ. Indians who lived on the mountain made caves, erected altars, prayed to the sun, and believed that the crest was the prison of all the evil spirits of the world. From its summit in 1609, they spied Henry Hudson's *Half Moon* on its maiden voyage up that beguiling river. In 1777, during the American Revolution, a beacon on the mountain warned American soldiers that British vessels were tacking up the stream. George Washington is supposed to have used the eyrie for mapping out a good deal of his Hudson River campaign; on the road at the foot of the mountain, Benedict Arnold met Major John Andre for their unfortunate rendezvous at nearby Treason House; night travelers on adjacent Storm King Highway often report seeing the ghost of General "Mad" Anthony Wayne riding his favorite horse.[24] It is a region steeped in history, legend, and the supernatural.

Owner and jealous watch dog of High Tor until his death on February 19, 1942, at the age of seventy-nine, was the gallant Elmer Van Orden. Way back before the American Revolution, King George III had given one of Elmer's Dutch ancestors a land grant that included the mountain; and successive generations of Van Ordens had owned the acres ever since. Half-way up the mountain, the bachelor recluse lived simply but enjoyably in an ancient one-and-a-half story farmhouse; he fetched his water from a spring near the house; and he chopped his own wood for fires. He worked his self-sustaining farm with the aid of his hired man and long-time companion August G. Weltie, who claimed to be a personal friend of Maxwell Anderson. For many years sundry traprock companies had pestered Van Orden to sell his mountain, but he always refused because he had no doubt heard how the quarriers had defaced nearby Mount Taurus for its road-building gravel. Before he would sell, he had to be certain that the buyer would not cut down his beloved peak; but still, as a foresighted conservationist, Elmer Van

Orden was unappreciated until Anderson's play appeared. When Burgess Meredith was rehearsing for his role as Van Dorn, the actor and a photographer struggled to the top of the Tor to take some publicity pictures; and, while up there, Meredith chanced to meet his odd neighbor for the first time (as mentioned earlier, Meredith resided in New City then). " 'What the hell are you doing here?' " the owner startled them by shouting. He was "pretty churlish about it all . . . doesn't like trespassers," continued the record of this confrontation.[25] At the mention of the stage play, the old man "snapped" that he had heard something about it; but he presently evinced some favorable interest in it by declaring, " 'I'd like to see that goddam show.' "

In March of 1937, not long after the "show" had opened in New York, Anderson and Meredith invited him to witness their interpretation of his way of life on the mountain. Van Orden donned his Sunday-best black suit, stuck a diamond stickpin into his antiquated tie, picked up his crook-handled black cane, and went to the Martin Beck Theatre where he chewed tobacco throughout a matinee performance. Afterwards, backstage, he argued amiably with Anderson about the play's conclusion; he contended that the hero should never have sold his land — and he never changed his view about the conclusion. His great-nephew William H. Van Orden said of his crusty forebear, perhaps exaggerating somewhat, that the play had made him " 'pretty mad.' "[26]

What finally happened to Van Orden's real High Tor that was so much endangered by traprock men? In 1943, thanks to a fund-raising campaign, the Hudson River Conservation Society and the Rockland County Conservation Association, of which Maxwell Anderson was a member, bought the entire Van Orden property from his heirs for twelve thousand dollars and then donated the twenty-three acres on the summit of High Tor to the Palisades Interstate Park where they are now secure.[27]

The main plot of *High Tor* follows Van Van Dorn, an individualistic young man of Dutch descent who shuns conventional employment and shoots and fishes for a living. He rejects the offers of two knavish realtors, Biggs and Skimmerhorn, who are bent on swindling him out of his mountain retreat so that they can raze the place for its rock. Besides the main plot there are four subplots: (1) Philosophic old John, last of the local Indians, wants to make sure that he is buried on High Tor among the bones of his ancestors when he dies;

his friend Van has agreed to inter him there when the time comes. John's invocation to the sunset in the symbolic opening of the play is rich in nature imagery and was supposed to have been especially affecting in the original stage presentation. (2) Three conventionalized but funny gangsters, Dope, Elkus, and Buddy, have narrowly escaped to High Tor with twenty-five thousand dollars robbed from the Nanuet bank. This money soon falls into the sticky hands of Biggs and Skimmerhorn, who become lost on the mountain in the night and whose temptations lead them into hilariously amusing contretemps. (3) A ghostly crew of Dutchmen has been marooned on the mountain for centuries while plaintively awaiting the return of their ship *Onrust* to take them back to the cobblestone wharves of Holland; sometimes, in their futile resentment against the strangeness of the new age they perforce inhabit, they roll their bowling balls against the airplane beacon and smash it. But, unlike Henry Hudson's mysteriously silent crew in Irving's "Rip Van Winkle," two of these people talk with their appropriate counterparts among the mortals; however, none of these Dutchmen cast any magic spells although there are plenty of magical overtones and supernatural happenings. Among this group is the captain's lovely young wife, Lise, with whom Van has a poignantly brief love affair; she is wistful for home and a lost love; and, like the other ghosts, she is sadly thinning away with the years into a translucence that is itself of fleeting duration. On this last topic — the transiency of life — Maxwell Anderson assigns to her the most eloquently lyrical and delectable dramatic poetry that ever came from his pen:

> When you [Van] must walk the air,
> as all must walk it sometime, with a tread
> that stirs no leaf, and breathe here with a breath
> that blows impalpable through smoke or cloud,
> when you are as I am, a bending wind
> along the grain, think of me sometimes . . .
> . . . .
> . . . For there comes a time
> When the great sun-lit pattern of the earth
> shakes like an image under water, darkens,
> dims, and the clearest voices that we knew
> are sunken bells, dead sullen under sea,
> receding.[28]

(4) The thinnest and least interesting story is about Van and his girlfriend Judith, who hesitates to marry him unless he has obtained a regular job and is earning money; by the close of the play and after Lise has vanished on the ship, Judith has given up her insistence on material security and she agrees to accept him as he is.

Van listens sympathetically to John's advice that "there's no hill worth a man's peace," and he arranges late in the play to sell his mountain to Skimmerhorn's father, a rather decent fellow, and to move westward with Judith where the land is wilder and the mountains bigger. Of course, all the various other plots end with a victory for the forces of honesty and patience, thanks to a skillful handling of coincidence and fanciful improbability: John is assured of an undisturbed grave site, the gangsters get arrested along with the realtors who had tried to pocket the stolen money, and the tardy *Onrust* at last rescues its spectral crew.

It seems to have been on the afternoon of a spring day about mid-March in 1936 that the germinal idea for *High Tor* first came to Maxwell Anderson.[29] He had climbed to the top of High Tor, and there, as he stood gazing upon the Hudson, he remembered "the Dutch fleet which had sailed up the river and . . . the Indians who had once dwelt on the mountain. By association the legend of Rip Van Winkle came to mind." The reporter or publicity agent to whom we are indebted for this information recorded the details from — in all likelihood — Anderson's own lips. And our unnamed source adds: "The phrase that came into his mind and began it all formed itself into something like this: 'A study of the evanescence of civilizations' . . . ." There is no reason to doubt that the inception of this new work occurred in at least approximately that way. The idea germinated in his mind for about two-and-one-half months before he began writing the first lines; a month after that, the labor was done.

An additional motivation behind *High Tor* came from Anderson's opposition to the quarrying which was taking place to the east and south of the actual mountain; the steam shovels, however, never reached the immediate area of High Tor. Anderson's son Quentin informed me by letter on May 17, 1971, about still another impetus behind the play, saying that, although quarrying indirectly threatened the real mountain, Anderson's indignation at the businessmen in the play might reflect even more so his feelings about an electric power company that was then planning to erect a high tension line over his beautiful waterfall; luckily for Maxwell Anderson, a neighbor foiled the company by building a house along the proposed route.

Since we know that the actual mountain inspired Maxwell Anderson's play, what about also the role of the unusual local owner, Van Orden? Danton Walker is mistaken in his assertion that Anderson before writing *High Tor* had neither met Van Orden nor been up the mountain where he lived.[30] Alan Anderson, who snorts at this assertion by Walker, claims that his father had been up the Tor numerous times beforehand; and, as we have seen, the newspaper account cited earlier covers one of those trips (it is not at all hard to climb the mountain). Furthermore, Alan says that his father knew Van Orden beforehand also, "visited him at least several times over the years," and "saw him at occasional neighborhood gatherings. . . ."[31]

Supporting Alan's contention are Van Orden's invitation to the theater, the hired man's claim to friendship with the playwright, and Maxwell Anderson's own active interest in local conservation affecting the mountain in question.[32] Van Orden's influence upon the play text is clearly noticeable in the use of the Dutch name Van Dorn, the identical locality, the importunities of the traprock people, and the living off the land in crusty independence. What little we learn about Van Dorn's Pap reminds us strongly of Van Orden; and, this being the case, Van Dorn is likely patterned after the kind of son that Van Orden might have had (but did not), a son reared close to nature, taught to be independent, and encouraged to share his father's devotion to the Tor.

Nonetheless, the characterization of Van Dorn suggests another equally strong probable source: the life and writings of Henry David Thoreau as these are set forth in his *Walden*. Some of the ways in which Anderson's hero may be considered a Thoreau figure include his aversion to routine or conventional employments; his pride in having to work only a few weeks of the year in order to earn enough for his annual support; his unsatisfying experience at laboring in a factory (Thoreau's stint in the family pencil factory); his ability to find complete sustenance on the land he occupies; his numerous skills, evidently manual ones; his belief that a man should not sacrifice the best part of his life in order to earn money so that he can retire much later; his indifference to luxuries and other material possessions; his scorn for needless travel; his distrust of government;

his interest in Indian life and legends; his love for natural beauty and wilderness scenes; his fondness for animals; and his contentment in living in a cabin alone — or until Judith consents to marriage. Just as Thoreau finally left Walden Pond for good, so does our hero at High Tor; but he leaves for a vastly different reason. The real Thoreau, of course, would never have sold that mountain.

The original for Lise might be Amy Murray, for whose poetry collection — *November Hereabout* (New York, 1940) — Maxwell Anderson wrote a charming preface that supplies the following significant information in which parallels may be found between the fictional and the real woman. For many years his friend and neighbor in Rockland County, Amy, like Lise, cultivated a flower garden (the poetess' garden was said to be the finest for miles around); she was in her youth very beautiful and from an alien land (Scotland); she sang well; she took a strong interest in legend, via Gaelic songs; and she made her most distinctive utterance in poetry.

Although some critics have aptly called *High Tor* poetic fantasy, the piece defies any settled classification: it is also a melodrama, a problem play, a romantic comedy, a low comedy, and a satire. These elements are intermixed, as we have seen, into a clever and complex plot structure; the result is an entertainment far subtler and more original than Jordan Miller implied when he labeled *High Tor* an "acceptable tour de force."[33] Anderson's thematic objective for the play as " 'A study of the evanescence of civilizations' " proves to be wholly consonant with what he does with his Van Dorn, John, and the Dutchmen as a whole. Each of these three groupings represents a cultural stage in history that is threatened with extinction; and their common plight unites the various parts of the story. Barrett Clark and George Freedley have together expressed a nearly perfect statement of what the sensitive reader finds in *High Tor*: ". . . the nostalgia of the poet for fair things past and dead, and the anger of the citizen who sees greed personified in the unimaginative hogs who would despoil beauty for financial gain."[34]

One of the drama's satirical political thrusts is aimed at Franklin Delano Roosevelt's New Deal administration that had come to power three years before. In Act I, Scene i, Anderson takes his first public swipe at it with James Aloysius Farley (1888–1976), the Democratic party leader from Anderson's own Rockland County whose activities were heavily responsible for Roosevelt's presidential election (afterwards, Roosevelt made him Postmaster General).

As the New Deal wore on, Anderson became increasingly critical; but, when *High Tor* was being conceived, he had not much cause for apprehension.[35] Much more prevalent than the political is the social satire in the drama, and we can see it in Van's comments about the worship of the automobile and about how he simply abandoned his own car in front of the police station one day; there is also satire about the restrictiveness of burial regulations and about the senseless desecration of natural beauty by businessmen driven solely by the profit motive. Anderson wins many a chuckle by allowing us to glimpse how odd our modern styles and customs are when examined through the seventeenth-century eyes of the minor character DeWitt to whom sandwiches are witches' food and paper money is "wishing paper."

Gassner does not exaggerate when he praises this work as containing "some of the best satire in English poetic drama since *The Beggar's Opera. . . .*"[36] Though the play says sharp things about the strange and materialistic course of American civilization, the satire never grows heavy; there is a vast deal of fun for its own sake. As a comic play, *High Tor* is one of the most outstanding examples of Anderson's talent for assimilating and transforming for his own uses some of the almost forgotten devices of dramatic art. In this connection, George R. Kenodle reminds us that the steam shovel for lifting the shysters aloft to their position of embarrassing exposure hearkens back to the Greek crane used by Aristophanes to put his Socrates into the air.[37] Almost anyone familiar with *The Tempest* will enjoy even more the burlesque situation in Act I, Scene iii, in which DeWitt chances upon the covered forms of the two sleeping realtors and asks aloud what strange creature of four legs is lying there.

Anderson has learned to perfection the technique illustrated in *The Tempest* and in *A Midsummer Night's Dream* of arranging the action so that the characters are separated into appropriate social groupings much of the time; and in such scenes the "high" characters use poetry among themselves for serious or elevated discourse; the "low" characters invariably use prose; and, when a "high" one happens to speak with a "low" one, he condescends to the other's use of prose. Moreover, other distinctions are observed even within social groupings: just as among Shakespeare's supernatural figures, the crude Caliban who speaks in prose (usually) and the delicate Ariel who speaks in poetry, Anderson's DeWitt and Lise are similarly differentiated. But such technique is far from being an original imitation or pastiche; it had been part of the Elizabethan heritage which Shakespeare freely used after learning it from the plays of George Peele and others.

One of the features of outstanding literature is supposed to be the final but unanswered mystery of character or situation — the hitherto unprobed depth — that remains to divert the reader after the author has closed his performance. In *High Tor*, for example, we never learn whether certain mortals had a dream about Dutch phantoms on the mountain — the uncovered seven graves of white people, including one woman, make us suspect that the dream, if any, was supernatural — or whether dream and reality interblended much in the way Lise explains to Van (she says that "spectres of an old time" still haunt the Tor), or whether her tale to him in Act II, Scene ii, about the king's inscribed goblet bears the answer.

Most of the important contemporary reviewers, including John Mason Brown, Brooks Atkinson, and Stark Young, were mightily pleased with this art, and a fair number of subsequent commentators have treated it as a modern classic. *High Tor* is easily the most perfect poetic fantasy yet written in the American theater.

VI The Star-Wagon

Fantasy also inheres in *The Star-Wagon* (1937), but it is science fantasy this time. One hobby of Maxwell Anderson's not divulged thus far in this book was science: Alan volunteers that his father "read a lot of it and tried to understand it all and tried to invent things. It fascinated him."[38] This hobby could have had an inspirational role in creating *The Star-Wagon*. Also, Anderson almost surely was familiar — if only through hearsay — with H. G. Wells' long-time popular novel *The Time Machine* (1895), or with its imitations, and with the famous scientific romances of Jules Verne. *The Star-Wagon*, which Anderson himself called a "potboiler,"[39] contains many of the ingredients of the popular type of Broadway stage fare, such as humor, sentiment, a touch of sex, music, readily identifiable characters, a story showing the aspirations of the common man, and an affirmation of the values of true love after the common man has had his fling.

Stephen Minch, the poor, unassuming industrial scientist in *The Star-Wagon*, invents a machine that carries him and his quaint friend Hanus Wicks back many years in time so that Stephen can discover whether he might have been happier had he married, instead of the Martha he now loves, the rich "other girl" who was so physically attractive. He weds the "other girl," but the union proves to be a disaster: wealth taints his character and hurts his friendship with Hanus. Disgusted after some years with this wasted life, he and Hanus return to the present where, strange to say, only a few hours have elapsed. Past has blended even more with present when they learn that Mrs. Martha Minch and also Stephen's boss at the plant had had their own separate dreams during the preceding night, dreams that had interpenetrated with the very time machine fantasy that Stephen and Hanus had experienced. The story ends happily in that the boss will promote Stephen to consulting engineer at a high salary.[40]

Despite the surface ordinariness of Stephen and Hanus, they are actually quite interesting and amusing people who quickly gain our respect. We admire and respect Stephen for his insistence on keeping himself independent as a worker, his deep-felt joy in tinkering and inventing, his disavowal of the profit motive that hamstrings so many creative minds, and his impractical generosity in disposing of his products. Alan Anderson says that his father based these characters "on a couple of old friends here in Rockland County [presumably Lloyd Orser and Carroll French, a carpenter-mason and a sculptor, respectively], and on his own affection for honest, muddling, good people as opposed to efficient, successful and somewhat ruthless and cold people."[41] Maxwell Anderson's love for the type shines through in the scene in which Stephen seriously accepts his boss's order to develop an improved automobile tire, devises one with a tread that resists a hundred and thirty thousand miles of wear! — and is accused by his boss of trying to wreck the tire industry which depends upon replacements! Act II, Scene ii, is so warm and comfortable and rich in nostalgia that it seems as if transcribed directly from the author's memory of his boyhood days when he had a variety of church choir experiences, including pumping by hand a church organ in Jefferson, Ohio.[42] In the passage just referred to, we are placed by the time machine in a town in Eastern Ohio, the time 1902, where the choir sings in the church loft and Hanus pumps the pipe organ for the officious Mrs. Rutledge.

Thanks to their quest with the time machine, Anderson's two heroes realize one of the fondest dreams of mankind — learning whether another role in life might bring them more happiness; but

Stephen's pessimism in the closing scene (Act III, Scene ii) signifies that men would simply make a bigger mess if they could do so. We are asked there to believe that good and bad fortune do not exist and that everything is for the best in this best of all possible lives (strikingly Emersonian ideas). However, the last six pages of this scene, where the melodrama grows intense, are difficult to accept for their thought content. As we know from the time journeys, Stephen would have been corrupted by wealth; but, returned, he is presumably happier because his salary has been raised to two hundred dollars a week. Stephen also tells Martha, on the basis of his bizarre travel experience, that people do not basically change; however, since he has obviously become wiser as the result of his experiences, a rationale for promoting time travel exists but, instead, such activity is presented as useless or worse. In fact, no one in this scene mentions even one of the many specific practical advantages of time travel. Quite, quite absent is man's daring spirit which d'Alcala in *Key Largo* prophesies is going on a conquest among the stars and planets. Maxwell Anderson is evidently forcing the play to a conclusion in which all things return to a safe status quo and in which no embarrassing technological devices are left lying around in the wrong hands.

Finally, when Hanus pumps an imaginary organ, Stephen and Martha join him in singing a fond old church hymn together; and the heavenly city of Zion yearned for and celebrated in the hymn they sing might suggest to some *other* person a glorious time trip to Zion someday, if only to see whether it exists; but this possibility is unvoiced, and with it go seemingly all serious implications. Moreover, the play ends with Stephen's making a lovely comparison between the shortness of their lives and that in Bede's story of the bird who flew out of the dark night, through a candle-lit room, and then out through another window. Stephen's sad and philosophic rejection of the magic machine, with which he can at will recover his youth with all its mad and foolish passions, is wonderfully reminiscent of what wise Dr. Heidegger concludes about his uses of the water of the Fountain of Youth in Nathaniel Hawthorne's short story "Dr. Heidegger's Experiment."

Soon after *The Star-Wagon* reached the Great White Way on September 29, 1937, Brooks Atkinson wrote two reviews about it for the *New York Times;* and he had apparently attended two different performances, for the two reviews indicate mixed reactions about the "hackneyed theme" of using a time device, about the "maundering and uneven" structure, and about the superiority of the scenes of the past over those of the present. Much more unfavorable was John Mason Brown; but, he too praised the acting that was no doubt responsible for keeping the play alive for two hundred and twenty-three nights. To George Jean Nathan, *The Star-Wagon* meant "complete banality, mushy and factitious sentiment" and "a piece of shoddy." Nathan was a little severe; for, unlike so many of Anderson's second- and third-rate plays, this one has a certain genuine feeling and a charm which no amount of carping can quite argue away.

VII   Bad Seed

No two popular Anderson plays could offer greater contrast than that found in the humor and warmth, the sentiment and nostalgia of *The Star-Wagon* as opposed to the surgical coolness and mounting horror of *Bad Seed*, which is unquestionably the final distinguished work of his old age. *Bad Seed*'s one set represents the apartment of Colonel Kenneth Penmark, his wife Christine, and their eight-year-old daughter Rhoda   the neat and pretty villain in this drama of terror. Upstairs lives their voluble friend Mrs. Monica Breedlove, who likes to expatiate about sex and psychoanalysis. As the story opens, Colonel Penmark departs for duty in Washington, D.C., and later in the day Rhoda leaves on a school picnic. For lunch, Christine entertains Reginald Tasker, a writer of mystery stories and a minor expert in criminology, who chances to describe the case of the sensational murderess Bessie Denker; and Christine starts when she hears this name. Later, the radio announces that little Claude Daigle had drowned that afternoon at the school picnic mentioned earlier. When Rhoda returns, she is strangely unmoved by the death of her classmate; and noticing this coldness, the building's spiteful and sadistic janitor, Leroy, teases her privately about it.

That evening Christine receives a telephone call from her father, Richard Bravo, a news correspondent who is coming to visit; because she is distraught by the reappearance of an old bad dream, she begs him to tell her whether there is some terrible thing in her past that she is unaware of; she has always felt she was adopted. Bravo, however, evades giving her an answer. A few days later, Miss Fern, head of the school Rhoda attends, drops by and tells Christine that

an older student had seen Rhoda grab at the penmanship medal won
by Claude and pursue him toward the wharf where he was later
found bruised and drowned. She believes that Rhoda is innocent
but is withholding information. Mrs. Daigle, tipsy and grieving,
arrives wanting to learn about the final minutes before Claude's
death — Rhoda was clearly the last person to see him alive.
Moreover, someone took the medal from Claude's shirt. The telephone rings when Mrs. Daigle leaves, and Christine chats long-
distance with Kenneth; she does not trouble him with her doubts;
and from then on she keeps him ignorant about the diabolical
events.

Christine soon happens to find the penmanship medal hidden in
the girl's table drawer; but, upon confronting Rhoda with the item,
she gets only a devious reply. When Christine reminds Rhoda of old
Mrs. Post, their acquaintance in Baltimore where they used to live,
who had died "accidentally" by falling down some stairs after she
had promised the little girl a certain crystal ball which Rhoda had
duly asked for and had received once the woman had died, Rhoda
assures her mother that the death was an accident. The first of the
play's two acts ends with Christine unwilling to believe, in the face
of all the evidence, that her acquisitive and cold-hearted daughter
bears any guilt at all. But she now has doubts.

Later that afternoon, after Rhoda opens a carton, Leroy comes in
to pick up the excelsior packing which will, incidentally, make a bed
for him in the garage. This time he begins to torment Rhoda by
pretending to know that she had beaten Claude before drowning
him and by telling her that the police can identify the murder
weapon by testing it for blood stains. Alone with her mother, the
now frightened Rhoda wants to know about the test; and she breaks
into tears when Christine says that she does not know the answer
but *will ask someone else*. That day, when Tasker arrives for
cocktails, the now thoroughly suspicious Christine pretends that she
is writing a novel so that she can learn from him whether or not
children commit murders. They do commit them, he says. Bravo at
last arrives and joins in the conversation; he had once written news
articles about the Bessie Denker case. When Christine asks if criminal children are always the product of environment, Tasker answers
no and Bravo *yes*, but the latter is suspiciously eager to change the
subject. Tasker again mentions Bessie Denker; and his description
of her beauty and charm, her convincing appearance of virtue, and

her extreme youth at the outset of her murderous rampage suggest Rhoda's very situation. Some people, he says, are "bad seeds" — inevitably bad because of heredity.

When Christine is alone with her father, she staggers him by saying that she fears Rhoda has done something dreadful but gives no details; and he responds by admitting that he had adopted Christine when she was less than two years old. Dark secrets emerge in their tête-à-tête. She tells him of her fearful dream — or is it re- membrance? — about escaping the clutches of a gracious, lovely woman, who had already killed one of the children, by sneaking out of the house and by hiding in weeds until neighbors rescued her. At hearing Christine's story, Bravo reveals that he had adopted the tiny Ingold Denker, the daughter of the murderess Bessie, and had changed her name to Christine. He is quite certain, even so, that the mother's criminality cannot be inherited and that Rhoda is a perfectly sound and sweet little girl.

After Bravo retires for the night, Christine spies her daughter carrying a suspicious-looking package to the incinerator chute; and, when she tries to take it from her, the child kicks and bites savagely. The package then rips open to reveal the death weapon, Rhoda's cleated shoes that she had used to kill Claude. Cornered now, the girl confesses but shows not an iota of remorse; she holds that the boy was entirely at fault simply for refusing her the medal. Seeing that her mother is profoundly shocked, Rhoda tries out her coquet- tish flattery — that she has, oh! the prettiest, the nicest, the sweetest mother! This time Christine will not be hoodwinked; but she tells her daughter to incinerate the shoes and to keep quiet.

The next morning, Leroy taunts the girl by mentioning a certain pink electric chair kept for little murderesses; he even guesses that she had beaten Claude with the shoes; and he arouses her hatred and fear by pretending that he had salvaged the shoes from the furnace. Rhoda reports to her mother what Leroy had said; but, before Christine can act, her father and Monica enter the room; and events rush to a crisis. Rhoda steals some matches and slips downstairs, ostensibly to buy a "popsickle." Grief-tortured and piti- fully drunk Mrs. Daigle reappears, this time more convinced than ever that Rhoda has not told all she knows. When Rhoda returns, an affecting scene occurs in which Mrs. Daigle kisses the murderer of her son and asks her why she wanted Claude's medal; and Rhoda coolly retorts that she wants to resume licking her "popsickle"!

Suddenly, screams of "Fire!" are heard; Leroy's garage room is aflame; a door locked from the outside has trapped him. Christine and Monica at the apartment window provide a report of Leroy's horrifying exit, his clothes and hair on fire, as he races screaming for the pond. Meanwhile, in the den, pretty Rhoda calmly practices "Au Clair de la Lune" on the piano — one of several brilliant touches by Maxwell Anderson, who did not find this one in William March's novel which forms the basis of the play.[43] Christine, hearing the piano, shrieks and shrieks for Rhoda to stop: she has reached her emotional breaking point.

That evening, while hearing a bedtime story, Rhoda admits to her mother that she killed Leroy because he would otherwise tell the police. She had set fire to the excelsior. Christine loves the daughter too much to allow some institution to take her away, but she cannot accept the horrors any longer; her recourse is to administer sleeping pills to her "baby," carry her off gently to bed, and then shoot herself. Some days later, Colonel Penmark is back and talking sorrowfully with neighbors and friends; he learns that Monica and her brother had rushed downstairs immediately after hearing the shot. Tasker recalls that Bravo had suddenly died of a heart attack after hearing of his daughter's death. None of those present have any idea why Christine fed Rhoda the pills and then killed herself, not even Monica with her psychology. That Rhoda is still living becomes all too apparent, shockingly so to the theater audience — but to the delight of those assembled with Colonel Penmark — when from the den issue the tinkling sounds of "Au Clair de la Lune"! Called, she emerges wreathed in smiles and lavishes on her unsuspecting but loving father her fatal, winning coquetry. Thus the "bad seed" lives on, despite all, scot free to murder again perhaps.[44]

It was the third Mrs. Anderson [*née* Gilda Oakleaf] who urged the then hospitalized playwright to transform March's popular thriller *The Bad Seed* into play form.[45] Anderson's illness did not impede his work, either in finish or ease of construction; for, after he had completed *Bad Seed* two months later[46] and in time for its presentation by The Playwrights' Producing Company in late 1954, many critics rated his adaptation as an artistic victory — as it chanced, the last one he was ever to enjoy in the theater. The improvements he made in the story that he found in the novel are too numerous and, in some instances, too subtle to cover here completely. He hewed to the basic plot of the criminal child who is motivated in her murders by her desire for possessions and by self-defense; he followed the same sequence of three crimes, even used the same character names; but he succeeded in removing so much clutter that the story moves with the simplicity and inevitability of Sophoclean tragedy.[47] And, like Oedipus, Christine's fate hinges upon her discovery of her own identity. Anderson also used one Fern sister instead of three, reduced Mrs. Daigle's three visits to two, eliminated Mrs. Forsythe and Miss Glass completely, omitted the parts about Leroy's home life, whittled down Monica's psychiatric chatter to a tolerable level (lest, as a comic figure, she detract from the serious material), and pruned away much from Bessie Denker's career.

Still more noticeable and important is the change that Anderson made relative to Bravo, who is dead in the novel but has a key role in the play, for Anderson's Christine confides her fears to Bravo only; but, in the novel, March's Christine, implausibly, tells her problems to no one except in unmailed letters to Mr. Penmark. Mr. Penmark enters only once in the novel, at the very end — clearly an awkward oversight for William March — but he figures in both the opening and closing scenes of the play where he is a slight yet more humanized figure. March makes him a businessman; but Anderson, who makes him a military officer, lends more believability to his sudden and extended absence from the apartment.

Anderson made his biggest changes in the depiction of Christine and Rhoda. Christine, as Mabel Bailey tells us, is "just the sort of person who would easily believe Tasker's explanation" regardless of how suspect the idea of inherited criminality is with modern psychologists. Moreover, Bailey thinks the tragic outcome would have been the same either way, for she would still try to destroy the child rather than yield her to some institution.[48] If a weakness exists in Anderson's depiction and use of this woman, as compared with March's, it is due to his rushing her a little too fast into a solution for her problem. Anderson has stripped away so much material from this phase of the story that the process of decision becomes telescoped, surgically neat, almost too simple considering the loving devotion that she has for her "baby" and husband. (The novel's Christine is rather self-centered in her brooding over Rhoda's guilt — is repelled by the girl.) Such a woman might hesitate more than she does in making up her mind and at least confide in her loving husband, as well as her father, say by telephone or letter. As it is, we are asked to believe that she would willingly have Colonel Pen-

mark, whose respect she values, think of her afterwards as a senseless murderer of the child they both love.

The Rhoda in the novel is cold, self-sufficient, practical, shows
little affection, and does not know how to feign affection; as such,
she is less likely to succeed in covering up her real feelings and
thoughts in order to escape detection. Moreover, because she is not
personable, she is that much less insidious and dangerous than Anderson's pretty Rhoda of the charming airs. Rhoda in *Bad Seed*, by
comparison, is definitely attractive; and the disparity between her
endearing coquettishness and basically evil nature contributes much
to the vividness of characterization.

Bad Seed departs from one of Anderson's rules for playwriting
which requires that evil not triumph at the end, but it follows nicely
the other rules. The reader of the play and the novel cannot help
noticing that Anderson borrowed intact from the novel the shock at
the end of having Rhoda survive her gentle mother because of a
timely rescue. This particular technique is not consistent with
tragedy; it lacks inevitability, and it belongs in the realm of melodrama. Nonetheless, the play reads well, despite all real or conjec-
tural shortcomings. Of course, Christine, not Rhoda, is the central
tragic figure; and it cannot be otherwise according to Anderson's
own tragic formula since Rhoda, in being genetically unable to make
moral decisions, is also unable because of her heredity to change for
the better in any way — at least in the story. Although a static figure
in this sense, Rhoda does manage to raise anew the fascinating,
age-old problem of "original sin." And we are left with the suspense
of not knowing *for sure* how much effect, if any, good environment
could eventually have in offsetting her bad heredity. But we are
loath to make any bets on *this* little girl. Anderson certainly does not
give himself enough credit when he calls this late adaptation of his a
"potboiler."[49]

From the plays studied in this chapter, we should recognize that
some of the versatile Anderson's most distinguished work does not
fit into the genres of war or historical drama and that of this group of
plays we have just discussed, *Winterset* and *High Tor* are preemi-
nent. As is true of so many of the outstanding plays covered in the
earlier chapters, the style is characteristically poetic; and the narrative is a serious one in which the idealistic hero or heroine is marked
for some kind of self-willed defeat for the sake, usually, of a worth-

while cause. To Elmer Rice, this situation develops because of Anderson's alleged "stringent religious indoctrination" early in life; because he has a "crucifixion complex, an obsession with the concept of martyrdom, as a listing of his protagonists clearly shows." Rice accordingly lists Jesus (though Anderson does not treat with his death), Sacco and Vanzetti, Medea (Oparre), as well as Socrates, Joan of Arc, Mary Stuart, Anne Boleyn, Essex, and certain heroes in *The Eve of St. Mark* and *Key Largo;*[50] and Rice could have added Margaret, Miriamne, and Van Dorn. But, as said earlier, Anderson strongly resisted religious indoctrination and early became an agnostic; therefore, it does little to account for the twist which the plays take and which is actually nothing new to world tragedy. This so-called "crucifixion complex" is found in *Oedipus Rex*, in all those Shakespearean tragedies where a hero commits suicide, and in *Death of a Salesman*. In short, what Rice damns with a psychiatric label is a non-essential but familiar feature of tragedy. What he omits to tell us is that Anderson was from the beginning a close student of classical drama, and moreover suffered enough firings for his convictions — at a young age when he was still most impressionable — to account to some extent for his tragic view of life.

CHAPTER 5

Conclusions

I The Developing Romantic

V ARIOUS as Anderson's contributions to the stage are, his choice of subject matter and his dramatic treatment are Romantic in a surprising number of instances; and this choice applies to practically all of his finest and most famous plays. He has a marked penchant for remote ages, for lost battles and lost causes, for colorful figures of history, for heroic gestures even on the brink of the grave, for the pomp and circumstance of royal pageantry, for famous love affairs in the palaces of nobles, for fantasy that brushes its velvet wings against the calico lives of ordinary people, and for dialogue that lifts the imagination on the soaring cadences of lofty rhetoric and lyric verse. Nonetheless, Anderson is a Realist when he applies modern psychology to his historic figures, when he presents the believable idealist who is caught amidst the crushing forces of power politics and what is euphemistically called "progress," and when he handles certain contemporary social problems such as marriage, racial and religious prejudice, political justice, and the role of heredity. But Anderson is overwhelmingly a Romantic. He detested this label[1] as much as he did that of historical dramatist; and he no doubt disliked it because he was such a versatile man of the theater and because he made so many alterations in the persons and stories of history. Moreover, no creative artist likes to be typed.

Anderson's career in the professional theater generally resolves itself into the following three periods: 1923–29 Collaborator and Apprentice; 1930–38 — Successful Poetic Dramatist and Political Idealist; and 1939–59 — Realist and Defender of Democracy. This classification tends to over-simplify a greatly varied career, especially with reference to the third period; but it serves most purposes of discussion. In his first period as an apprentice and collaborator, he joined with a succession of co-authors in essaying first one type of popular work and then another in his search for material and artistic success; and he failed at almost all. The poetic tragedy "White Desert," though a failure in most respects, pointed the way that he yearned and needed to go; but his development as a dramatic poet was tardy. Until well into the second period, he delayed using the ornaments of imagination and also any rhythms that were conscious and clear-cut; indeed, he was so cautious that his verse was usually undistinguished and resembled polished prose. Despite a strong but short interest in Socialism (outgrown by the 1930's), he ventured into left-wing drama only briefly and from then onward kept whatever nondidactic "message" was in his plays subordinated to literary art; for both his tragic view of life and his exalted aims as a playwright made proletarian drama uncongenial to him.

With *Elizabeth the Queen*, he happily wove into a single fabric his loves for poetry, tragedy, history, and romance; and he thus began creating his main cluster of poetic dramas for which he is best known today. These dramas have complex characters who partake of the vitality of life. The complexity of these characters develops unevenly from play to play, like the quality of the poetry, and reaches its maximum growth in *Winterset*. In this prolific second period, he triumphed as an artist — as practically all critics agree; but the triumph was not due alone to his discovery at or about the time of *Mary of Scotland* of his serviceable tragic formula that he modeled on Aristotle but also to his complex heroes and heroines and to his no longer severe but imaginative poetry which is sometimes lyric and sometimes meditative. The typical protagonists in the dramas of the 1930's have a political idealism locked in bitter conflict with the corruption of power. They confront a dilemma: on the one hand, given their idealism, individual fulfillment is impossible in a sphere in which a jealous and calculating self-interest rules its leaders; but, on the other hand, such central characters are impelled to pursue the ideal even if it brings them an inevitable defeat.

The reader of such works is thus led to conclude that it is far wiser to die young — at least, vicariously — while being grandly defiant in a good cause and unstained in character than it is to drag out the years and grow hardened and cunning in a world antithetical to honor and justice, truth and good faith. Given such a scurvy set of conditions, we easily see how the Hamlet figure develops in the plays even without need of Shakespeare's inspiration. Although the influence of Shakespeare is nonetheless strongest in this second period, more so in *Elizabeth the Queen* than in later works, it did not seriously diminish Anderson's originality. Even so, Anderson, unlike many other and lesser dramatists of this century and later, will probably be unfairly linked with Shakespeare and accused of such deficiencies as imitativeness of Elizabethan style.

Significant changes took place in the late 1930's, one of which was that Anderson discontinued for the most part his dramatic poetry, probably for two reasons: (1) he recognized that his poetry was not so good as his prose, and (2) the verse dramas, though they earned him money, did not usually pay well. Consequently, he turned his hand to writing a variety of prose plays in order to achieve, among other things, a higher or a steadier income. Starting with the 1939 revision of *Both Your Houses*, Anderson's ideology shifted toward an accommodation with actual contemporary conditions; and the evidence of shift is found in his consciously patriotic war plays, few of which amounted to anything as art. In this connection, Anderson assuredly grew as a man and patriot; but, with few exceptions, he declined as an artist.

This period also witnessed, however, another development in Anderson's work — the power of love. Some critics have indicated the frequency of love relationships in his dramas; and a handful of others — mainly Avery in "Maxwell Anderson: A Changing Attitude toward Love"[2] — have commented about the power that love has to elevate men and women to unwonted heights. Avery has shown, for the most part convincingly, that this concept of love is the first of several stages: (A) In the 1920's and 1930's, love is Romantic in the form of sublimated sex in the plays. (B) In the 1940's, love can still ennoble and inspire; but now, thanks at least partly to the author's contact with military life where he marveled at the soldiers' preoccupation with sex, love includes an interest in the biological, the physical aspects, that we find in *Anne of the Thousand Days*. I maintain, however, that Anderson's growing use of such sexual material is paralleled by other popular dramatists of the era whose mutual influence one upon the other cannot be ignored. As a practical man of the theater, he naturally tried to keep up-to-date. (C) In the 1950's, such sentimental notions as Anderson had formerly entertained about love, which is to say sexual passion, are now satirized, at least in the unpublished "Madonna and Child" (1956), which is presumably representative of how he then felt.

II *Ideas on Philosophy, History, and Government*

Anderson's cosmic philosophy is not, of course, systematic; and though he probably never thought of himself as a philosopher, he nevertheless voices some lofty strains of idealistic thought in the essay "Whatever Hope We Have" and in Act II of *Key Largo* where, as shown earlier, d'Alcala delivers to McCloud his inspiring message. To summarize, Anderson holds that the essence of man is not what he happens to be at a given time but what he imagines and wishes to become; that he lives his brief life journeying among the constellations where there is no certainty about the meaning of his life or destiny except for an occasional illumination provided by science or religious teachings, art, or the idealism of the young. Anderson finds that certain great souls before us have set down their records of noble triumph or suffering or defeat — these commonly expressed as symbols — which are prophetic and moreover motivate men in the pursuit of a distant goal of aspiration for the race. What is acquired is a racial dream that mankind can finally improve itself in goodness and wisdom.

These spiritual views Anderson attributes in his essay (pp. 19–22) to what he has learned about the supreme achievements in poetry, music, graphic and plastic arts; in the Sermon on the Mount; and in the final chapter of Ecclesiastes. His idealism also owes something to the essays of Emerson; to one or more of the formal Existentialists, although he could easily have arrived at this cast of thought by reading any number of authors from Friedrich Nietzsche and Feodor Dostoevski onward; to the beautifully melancholy skepticism of Matthew Arnold, whom he read often; to his studies in science, which almost inexorably would have challenged the traditional Scriptural interpretation of the cosmos; to his father's Christian humanism, notwithstanding their formidable differences relative to theology; and to his own rebellious and idealistic temperament that refused to accept in the long twilight of the gods any eclipse of the human spirit.

Despite modern man's being so easily the victim of self-doubt and multiform restrictions upon his personal freedom and upon his influence in the body politic, Anderson felt that today's man has an obligation to assume some kind of heroic even though humble role in the active defense of justice, freedom, and tolerance; otherwise, if he does not, he is untrue to the best that lies in him. Yes, and man is to fulfill such a role without necessarily any comfort from traditional Christian supernaturalism and any hope of personal immortality. Despite being an agnostic, Anderson was nonetheless convinced of the tremendous importance of *some kind* of spiritual faith — lucky are those who have it — in a world threatened by tyranny; and he manifested this awareness in *Joan of Lorraine* and *Journey to Jerusalem*.

The publication of Hervey Allen's novel *Anthony Adverse* in mid-1933 revealed and in part stimulated a remarkable degree of public interest in books about history, especially Americana; and the decade is full of such best-sellers. Although Anderson with his plays had anticipated the vogue by several years, it is probably more than a coincidence that only after the vogue had begun did his own career as a historical dramatist get well underway. In such dramas as he prepared, he shows history to be, in the main, a sordid prison house where human liberty and love gasp for air; and he also signifies that no one can expect to learn an accurate historical account because a powerful ruler, an Elizabeth for example, could dictate what the surviving record would be. Thus, by implication, art may be just as valid as formal history — and maybe even more so. His Henry VIII affirms the superiority of the interpreter of events (the artist) over the mere chronicler where he says that the interpreter never writes down precisely what happened; yet, still, what he writes approaches the truth more closely than does what actually occurred or was spoken (*Anne of the Thousand Days* [Act II, Scene ii]). In addition, art can be vastly more real and interesting than formal history, even if the narrative is actually built on a quagmire of lies for which the artist is not himself altogether responsible. We can see this last situation in Anderson's unpublished "Richard and Anne" in which Anderson, whose setting is a contemporary staging of Shakespeare's *Richard III*, has ghosts of the original characters flit in and try to set the record straight. In this play, Henry VII is supposed to have rewritten the facts of history in order to vilify his predecessor Richard III, who, contrary to report, was not a monster at all; then Shakespeare had inherited the lies and had unashamedly wrought on them such a magical sea change that they now seem real (*Catalogue* [pp. 75–76]). Watching such shifting sands and mirages as the historical past affords, Anderson must have felt doubly free, even obligated, to transform as creatively as he desired some of the "facts" handed to him as he fashioned his so-called "history" plays;

but, like other writers, he usually shied away from violating what he could reasonably expect an audience to know already.

His idea that wealth and power corrupted a leader remained with him from early to late in his career, even when he commenced championing democratic government as the least of possible evils in statecraft. The prospects for the common man continued gloomy, at least up to 1942 when Anderson remarked to Robert Rice: " 'The only way the little man can be free is to keep the big boys — government, industry, labor; executive, legislative, judicial — scrapping among themselves. Then he can escape between their legs.' "[3] Anderson presented ample warning of how the American government is steadily and stealthily encroaching on the individual's rights and independence. In *Both Your Houses*, he unequivocally shows this development, and he has his Congressman Sol predict something about the vulnerable citizenry that is already turning out to be true — Americans fret about being over-taxed but are in reality only seeing the *beginning* of this legalized mulcting — just give the government a few more years! (Act III, Scene ii). In *Key Largo*, he points out the illusory benefits of the Federal Social Security Act of 1935; for this useful program (as most of us regard it) has nevertheless grown so shockingly expensive as to make many sober people question its fairness and efficiency.

But Anderson's satire gains its greatest current relevance in *Knickerbocker Holiday*. In this extravaganza, Anderson's attack on the strong-arm radicalism of Roosevelt, who boldly enlarged the powers of the executive branch of government, suggests by extension the criminal abuses of the Richard Nixon administration which perpetrated, among other numerous scandals, the White House conspiracy and cover-up — the "Watergate" affair. The very fact that Nixon unashamedly and publicly referred to the president as the "sovereign" who had the right to break laws in the interest of national security[4] is glaring proof that our playwright's fears about the menace of big government were well founded after all. Finally, Anderson was one of the earliest and most vocal of artists to warn us about the dangers of Hitler and Franco, and about how even idealistic revolutions in France and Russia could fail.

III *Accommodation to Broadway*

Anderson's good fortune with some of his serious and unconventional dramas must have helped convince him that quality work could be done on Broadway despite its overweening preference, its near-mania, for the long-run play that frequently is a lightweight comedy or spectacular musical. Dorothy Thompson wrote to him for his assistance in starting a repertory theater, but he refused her on the grounds that his own scope, for instance, had not been cramped under the New York conditions and that the theater she proposed would *not be remunerative* and would therefore fail.[5] (He distrusted government- and public-supported theater.) This letter may explain the crux of Anderson's motivations and the source of a few of his shortcomings as a writer — his desire, albeit genuine, to secure the integrity of his art at the same time that he made that art pay well on his one market, the stage, where it could do so. He was not one to rest on posthumous laurels and at the same time forgo immediate earnings. We do not mean to say that he was money hungry; but, having become accustomed to big returns over the years, and having almost never gambled on a play for the experimental theater, he must have found it most difficult and probably even demeaning to imagine his drama as destined for any place but Manhattan, the most obvious focal point of stage success in the nation, where he could reap the optimum cash reward.

Ironically, Anderson's faith in the taste of the general public, as opposed to that of the New York City critics, never grew so robust that he changed his market. Yet, in justification of his choice, he must have realized that he would have in such a big, central market, to which outlying districts look for material, a far greater influence — should it ever happen — in promoting poetic tragedy on the world stage. However, as things turned out, he formed neither a school nor a lasting tradition. Anderson did not always rest easy with the accommodation thus effected between art and commercial success; and, as he wrote at the zenith of his career to the wife of Professor Hult, he felt that his plays had suffered extensively from being created to satisfy a demand. Although fulfillment of this demand was the sole means by which plays could be profitably written, he quickly added that he had endeavored to strike a reasonable compromise between his work and his soul.[6] Perhaps if he had not built for himself a life dependent upon a high income, if he had dared more often to choose a less restricted and pampered audience than that on the Great White Way, and if he had risked more often the loss of an occasional royalty check, he conceivably would have created more fine plays than he did, but he wanted his work to gain an immediate acceptance and therefore (as he reasoned) assurance of survival.

Despite Anderson's heroic efforts year after year with dramatic poetry, he evinced a certain degree of hesitation in striking out in new directions — certainly after the 1930's — because he was perhaps so much the scholar-traditionalist. His hesitancy appears in the essay "By Way of Preface: The Theatre as Religion" where he notes what he considers an important difference between what poets and prophets on the one hand and what playwrights on the other can safely do. He reveals in this rationale no bold spirit of originality, like that in O'Neill. From Anderson's own dramatic practice, however, we recognize that he did upon occasion pursue the unconventional, as in *Winterset*. Despite his personal shyness, Anderson felt close ties with his immediate audience, whose approval he was willing to court up to a point, but only up to a point, for he was wary of prostituting his art.

In his essay that is significantly titled "Compromise and Keeping the Faith," he postulates that a drama worth producing must necessarily contain a "dream" which the writer can and must defend against all detractors; and yet, unless the writer is willing to permit almost any number of artistic concessions to the theatrical organization, he probably never will get his play performed.[7] This was Broadway, whose special demands he took pride in meeting; and, in so meeting them, he must have, as he hinted, sacrificed his art in some little details, even though he left the "dream" intact. *Joan of Lorraine* is about this kind of minimum compromise with expediency. But, throughout his career, Anderson exhibited beyond question an integrity that merited the respect of practically everyone who knew him.

What Anderson would have wrought had he followed the lead of Paul Green and Susan Glaspell by writing more or less exclusively for off-Broadway theaters and by not so directly and insistently seeking his fortune is difficult to imagine because of the lavish giving and living that he finally got used to and because of his need for certain incentives that Green and Glaspell, voluntarily or otherwise, did without. But we may feel sure that, could he have drawn a passable income from the off-Broadway stage, he would still have written the verse plays a few of which — notably *Elizabeth the Queen*, *Mary of Scotland*, *Valley Forge*, *High Tor*, and *Winterset* — constitute today his chief glory in the dramatic literature of the world. Yet the truth

is that commercial-minded Broadway, about which he finally suffered misgivings, somehow elicited much of his most valuable and
entertaining work.

IV *Comparisons with Other American Playwrights*

Before Maxwell Anderson, the three most notable practitioners of
poetic drama in America had been George Henry Boker (1823–90),
William Vaughn Moody (1869–1910), and Percy Wallace MacKaye
(1875–1956). Of these writers, Anderson most resembles MacKaye
whose career overlapped with his own: both began as school
teachers and went on to write musical works and fantasies; both
wrote plays about Washington, Joan of Arc, the English Renaissance, and Classical Greece; each showed in his art an indebtedness
to Shakespeare and Washington Irving (cf. MacKaye's opera *Rip
Van Winkle*); and both saw at least some of their work on Broadway,
though most of MacKaye's was intended for regional theaters. Anderson's contemporaries T. S. Eliot and Archibald MacLeish, who
wrote dramas in free verse, enjoyed a comparatively brief favor on
the stage; they might have fared better had they not rejected blank
verse as inappropriate to speech in twentieth-century plays; but
Anderson, to his credit, had the bravery and the talent to adapt it to
his own purposes — heedless of the reputed anachronism of using a
form declared out of vogue — and made it a sometimes flexible
instrument long accepted by audiences.

The fact that Robert E. Sherwood had mutually valuable relationships with Anderson in The Playwrights' Producing Company makes
the similarities of their careers of special interest to us, even though
Sherwood neither attempted nor mastered poetic drama, and even
though it may be difficult to demonstrate very many specific
influences of one upon the other beyond Sherwood's role in the
censorship of *Storm Operation* and Anderson's penning of a scene
for *Abe Lincoln in Illinois* at the request of Sherwood.[8] Both were
university-trained men who married several times, warned us in
their literature about the specter of World War II, undertook civilian, war-effort duties, and wrote film scenarios and rather unsuccessful television shows. Oddly enough, the earliest war play of each
was pacifistic; but, when totalitarianism threatened Europe, each
wrote an invasion drama — Sherwood, *There Shall Be No Night;*
Anderson, *Candle in the Wind* — that announced each playwright's

desire to fight aggression. However, likenesses in the subject matter of their other dramas exist: both wrote about the American Revolution, about the Americans fighting the Japanese in the Pacific during World War II, about a future American president, about a woman who tried to seduce a great general, about ancient Athens (Sherwood's "Acropolis" was never published), about murder at a highway cafe in the West, about a Hamlet figure (in Sherwood, he is Alan Squier of *The Petrified Forest*), and about gangsters on the run from the police. Like Anderson, Sherwood also won the Pulitzer Prize (three times); but he originated far fewer plays, many of which seem dated to us now. Sherwood's admiration for Roosevelt was, of course, something that his colleague did not share finally.

Despite these comparisons with other dramatists, Anderson was, on the whole, an isolated figure, partly for his singular aim as a poetic tragedian determined to make his art succeed with the masses, partly for the sheer bulk of his creations, and partly for the commercial success in which he outdid all of those just mentioned. His only superior in tragic drama in America was O'Neill, whom he surpassed, however, in having the crucial gift of poetry; therefore, Anderson's graceful dialogue lifts the spirit and imagination whereas O'Neill's does not. Anderson also surpassed him in versatility, for O'Neill had no talent for such genres as the comedy, the musical, and and the political satire. Otherwise, O'Neill exceeds him in originality of technique. Brooks Atkinson could well be right in his prophecy that, "When the history of American drama is exhumed from libraries in the next century, it is likely that O'Neill and Anderson will be the two names best known to the scribbling graverobbers of that dark age."[9]

V *Limitations and Significance*

A critic in 1938 unwittingly spoke for many in his observation that "[Maxwell Anderson] has a poet's heart, if not his song. . . ."[10] Much of Anderson's output corroborates this impression, unfortunately; the poetry is indeed greatly uneven in merit; and, though Anderson well knew that fact, he definitely did have the poet's song on occasion. If his verse had often been elsewhere as good as it was in some sections of *Key Largo* and more especially so in *Winterset* and in *High Tor*, where the imagery and fine feeling are impressive, he might have achieved the position of the great dramatic poet that he called for in "Poetry in the Theatre." Like Walt Whitman before him, he had pointed out an important vacancy to be filled in our literature; and like him, but with more modesty, he applied for it; regrettably, both showed more promise than fulfillment. Perhaps Anderson's lack of a firm religious belief accounts to some degree — as it does with O'Neill — for his failings as a tragedian; for all the tragic masters have had some kind of supernatural underpinning for their art.

In addition to Anderson's having an inconstant poetic gift and a religious skepticism, he also neglected to experiment in bold ways worthy of, say, O'Neill. Yet, when he did experiment, he arrived at such marvelous results as we find in *Winterset* and *High Tor*. He also made a mistake in not taking a cue from Tennessee Williams and Arthur Miller to broaden his base with what may well be the foremost accepted medium for stage tragedy in the future (as it seemingly already is) — the creation of prose in which the poetic atmosphere is achieved, for instance, with Expressionistic devices and effects. Anderson did use some of these techniques, for example in the dream scenes of *The Eve of St. Mark* and in the memory ones of *Anne of the Thousand Days*, but he began doing so too late in his career to make much difference in his prime work. When poetic effects were needed, his first and final choice was the traditional one of verse itself; and he also made this choice in all of his fantasies, except for *The Star-Wagon*.

Part of Anderson's significance in world drama is in proving to us many times over that the wonderful, time-honored tradition of poetic utterance can please the big modern audience just as it did in the glorious days of the Globe theater. He is to the American stage what Sean O'Casey is to the Irish, what Edmond Rostand is to the French, and what Johann Schiller is to the German. He is one of a handful of playwrights in the twentieth century who scaled the alpine heights of poetic drama, and he is also one of a still smaller group who reached the pinnacle of tragedy itself. Even those who do not enjoy Anderson's dramas will, I think, certainly admire his noble spirit, his high-mindedness, his unflagging courage, his devotion both to his country and to its best ideals of human liberty, and his singular dream of returning dramatic poetry to the theater.

Notes and References

Chapter One

1. Donald Heiney, *Recent American Literature* (Great Neck, N. Y., 1958), p. 369.

2. The material about the mother's painting pictures comes from Ruth W. Sedgwick, "Maxwell Anderson, Playwright and Poet," *Stage*, XIV (Oct., 1936), 55, and from the eleven-page set of notes furnished me by Mrs. Lela A. Chambers in her letter of Apr. 26, 1972, hereinafter referred to as Lela Chambers' Biographical Notes. These Biographical Notes, plus letters from Mrs. Chambers, tell about one of the mother's half-brothers, George J. Stephenson (born 1855), who became late in life a minor public entertainer for a Los Angeles radio station — singing gospel and secular songs.

Unless a published source or a private owner is mentioned, all letters to or from Anderson cited in this book are those which I have personally examined in the Maxwell Anderson collection at the University of Texas library; those letters labeled *Catalogue* are in the same collection and are at the same time described in Laurence G. Avery's *A Catalogue of the Maxwell Anderson Collection at the University of Texas* (Austin, Texas, 1968) which I rely upon for certain citations. Evidently the biggest collection of letters and other Anderson materials resides at the University of Texas. For a study of the holdings, see Laurence G. Avery's "The Maxwell Anderson Papers," *The Library Chronicle of the University of Texas*, VIII (Spring, 1965), 21–33. Other chief repositories of Andersonia include University of North Dakota; Library & Museum of the Performing Arts (New York Public Library); The State Historical Society of Wisconsin (Madison, Wisconsin); and Library of Congress.

3. This man, Samuel Anderson, had a son Samuel who settled in Crawford County, Penn., in 1796 and later served in the War of 1812 — on the American side. Unless otherwise indicated, I am indebted to Lela Chambers' Biographical Notes and to her letters to me for materials that relate to Anderson's family background, childhood, intellectual and social development, and home addresses during his pre-university days. Some items about his intellectual development come from his "Love Letter to a University," *North Dakota Quarterly*, XXXVIII (Winter, 1970), 89–90, which was

first printed in *University of North Dakota Alumni Review* (Dec. 5, 1958), and is hereinafter designated as "Love Letter."

4. Barbara Leifur, "Leading American Playwright UND Graduate," *Dakota Student* (University of North Dakota student newspaper), Mar. 7, 1956, p. 6. The article reads as if Leifur had had some kind of first-hand communication with Anderson.

5. Anderson letter of Nov. 1, 1938, to Louis Azrael.

6. Robert Rice, "Maxwell Anderson: A Character Study of the Most Talked of Playwright in America Based on the First Interview He Has Granted since 1937," *PM's Sunday Picture News*, III (Nov. 29, 1942), 24.

7. *Ibid*.

8. Anonymous, "Maxwell Anderson, Playwright, is Dead," *New York Times*, Mar. 1, 1959, I, 84 [hereinafter called "Obituary"]. Also, Lela Chambers' Biographical Notes. The children, with married names in brackets, and birthdates, are: Ethel Mae [Chambers], 1887; James Maxwell, 1888; Lela Blanch [Chambers], or commonly Lela Anderson [Chambers], 1890; Harold Alfred, 1892; Ruth Virginia [Duffy], 1897; John Kenneth, 1901; Dorothy Elizabeth, twin to John, 1901; Laurence, 1913. Therefore, in error are *Current Biography* (1942) and Robert Rice (23) where we read about four boys and girls in the family. Ethel Mae and Lela Blanch married brothers named Chambers.

9. Helen Deutsch, "A Playwright and Poet," *New York Herald Tribune*, Sept. 22, 1935, p. 1.

10. Robert Rice, "Maxwell Anderson: A Character Study . . . ," p. 23. See Anderson's poem "The Time When I was Plowing," included in his collection *You Who Have Dreams* (New York, 1925), p. 13, which seems a genuine evocation of his personal experience of laboring among the endless fields in the farm country. Lela Chambers says the location is the Haskett farm at Bottineau, N. D., where Anderson had worked for Margaret Haskett's father.

11. Lela Chambers in her Biographical Notes hints at eight; Robert Rice, who gets his figure directly from Anderson, says eleven; "Obituary," the least reliable source for such a detail, reports thirteen.

12. Maxwell Anderson's letter Feb. 17, 1943, quoted in Allan G. Halline's "Maxwell Anderson's Dramatic Theory," *American Literature*, XVI (May, 1944), 70.

13. Avery, "The Maxwell Anderson Papers," p. 23.

14. Sedgwick, p. 55. Maxwell Anderson, "Preface," *Four Verse Plays* (New York, 1959), p. vi.

15. Avery, "The Maxwell Anderson Papers," p. 26. Alan Anderson wrote to me — in two letters, Oct. 27 and Nov. 23, 1970, respectively — that his father considered Shakespeare "one of the greatest men who had ever lived — and there were few of them in his mind." And, "Keats was indeed one of his favorites. He never stopped re-reading him. . . ." On Anderson's admi-

ration for Shakespeare and Sophocles, see "Poetry in the Theatre," *Off Broadway Essays about the Theatre* (New York, 1947).

16. Anderson letter of Mar. 3, 1941 to the actress Helen Hayes.

17. "Love Letter," p. 90.

18. Robert Rice, p. 24.

19. Letter from Lela Chambers of Mar. 27, 1972 to me. Also, her Biographical Notes.

20. Letter from Alan Anderson of Jan. 15, 1972 to me.

21. Telephone interview with Alan Anderson on Mar. 12, 1972.

22. Much of the material I have used for the University of North Dakota experience is taken from "Love Letter"; also, from C. L. Robertson's "In the Days of Peg-Top Trousers" (pp. 52–54) and Louis G. Geiger and J. R. Ashton's "UND in the Era of Maxwell Anderson" (pp. 55–60), both of which appear in *The North Dakota Quarterly*, XXV (Spring, 1957). Exceptions to these three sources are noted wherever they occur.

23. Anonymous, untitled section in *Whittier College Bulletin*, XII (Aug., 1917), 8. Also, "Obituary."

24. On June 11, 1935, the Grand Forks *Herald* printed a poem by Anderson titled "1908–1935 (For F. H. Koch)" which commemorates his student life at the university there, particularly the classes he had with Koch. In this poem, he speaks approvingly of Koch's reading from R. W. Emerson and from Christopher Marlowe's *Tamburlaine*. Reprinted in *The Carolina Play-Book*, VIII (Sept., 1935), 85–86. Copy of poem supplied me through courtesy of John P. Hagan.

For Koch's career, see Samuel Selden's *Frederick Henry Koch, Pioneer Playmaker* (Chapel Hill, N. C., 1954) and Hagan's "Frederick Henry Koch and the American Folk Theatre," unpublished doctoral dissertation, Indiana University, 1969.

25. John P. Hagan, "Federick H. Koch and North Dakota: Theatre in the Wilderness," *North Dakota Quarterly*, XXXVIII (Winter, 1970), 78–79.

26. Of course, Green and Wolfe as students belong to the University of North Carolina phase that began when Koch moved there in 1918.

27. Hagan, "Federick H. Koch . . . Wilderness," p. 75, where he quotes from an unidentified speech or writing by Koch defending his dream of promoting regional drama.

28. Upon receiving the playbills of the first native plays of the Midwest, Anderson expressed to him great enthusiasm in his California letter, dated 1917. — Frederick H. Koch, "Making a Regional Drama," *Bulletin of the American Library Association*, XXVI (Aug., 1932), 468.

29. "Making a Regional Drama," p. 468. The characters in the play are natives to the North Dakota prairies, and the time is Dec., 1888, the month and year of the author's birth, hence a period somewhat familiar to him.

30. "Lost Labors Love" was written in collaboration with R. H. Montgomery. — Geiger and Ashton, p. 57. Also, Deutsch, p. 1.

31. "The Masque of Pedagogues," *North Dakota Quarterly*, XXV (Spring, 1957), 33–48. Complete re-print of the play.

32. Some of the inspiration to write plays could have come from an event reported by R. P. Wilkins in Editor's Notes of *North Dakota Quarterly*, XXXVIII (Winter, 1970), 91. Anderson saw at Grand Forks the superb Russian actress Alla Nazimova star in Henrik Ibsen's *A Doll's House*, said to be the first play he had ever seen acted by a professional company.

33. Walter Prichard Eaton, "He Put Poetry Back on the Stage," *New York Herald Tribune*, Jan. 28, 1934, p. 12.

34. "Socrates and His Gospel," Introduction to *Barefoot in Athens* (New York, 1951), p. viii.

35. Randall J. Buchanan, "A Playwright's Progress," *North Dakota Quarterly*, XXXVIII (Winter, 1970), 72.

36. Leifur, p. 6.

37. Letter of Alan Anderson, Jan. 15, 1972, to me.

38. Hesper, the fourth and last child, born 1934, is the child of Anderson's second marriage, to Gertrude (Mab) Maynard in 1933. After Gertrude's death in 1953, he married his third and last wife Gilda Oakleaf the next year. — Letter to me from Alan Anderson, Nov. 23, 1970, whose errors in dating I have corrected herein.

39. Leifur, p. 6. The principalship is confirmed in other published accounts.

40. See Anderson's letter to Professor John M. Gillette (Sept. 15, 1912), as excerpted by Wilkins, p. 4. Gillette, his former professor, converted him into a pacifist.

41. Wilkins, p. 4; Philip Stevenson, "Concerning M. Anderson: A Word about the Career and Thoughts of the War Dramatist," *New York Times*, Jan. 9, 1944, II, 1. But Lela Chambers in her Biographical Notes counters: "Max said nothing about this being the reason for his leaving Minnewaukan when he and Margaret and Quentin visited us in the summer of 1913."

42. Letter to me of Nov. 9, 1971, from Mrs. Susan R. Rosenberg, Asst. Archivist to Stanford University Libraries; also letter to me of Nov. 12, 1971, from Armista M. Cook, Office of the Registrar, Stanford University.

43. Unsigned sketches of new teachers in *Whittier College Bulletin* XII (Aug., 1917), 7–8. There is almost unanimous agreement among the few informants who give a dating for the Polytechnic High School phase — an obscure period for Anderson. Wilkins made an innocent slip in the *North Dakota Quarterly*, XXXVIII (Winter, 1970), 4, where he has Anderson teach at Polytechnic after, but apparently not before, the Whittier professorship. The *Whittier College Bulletin*, above, states that Anderson had already been three years in the San Francisco school. Moreover, Charles W. Cooper in his *Whittier: Independent College in California* (Los Angeles,

1967), p. 127, affirms that Anderson "had been teaching in San Francisco [prior to Whittier] . . . ." Cooper's letter of Feb. 1, 1972 to me backs up his statement in the book, in response to my query for confirmation; and he adds that Anderson's second residence in San Francisco was for the apparently sole purpose of writing for the *Bulletin* full-time. Supporting this view are Carl Carmer, "Maxwell Anderson Poet and Champion," *Theatre Arts Monthly*, XVII (June, 1933), 437; and Deutsch, p. 5, who had direct communication with him.

There is hardly any possibility tht Anderson taught at Polytechnic both before and after Whittier, because his sister Lela wrote to me in two letters — Mar. 27 and Apr. 14, 1972 — that "Max" taught only once at Polytechnic, and that by 1918 he was working exclusively on the San Francisco paper. The official San Francisco records, which pertained to teachers' lists prior to 1930, have been destroyed. — Letter to me from Robert C. Seymour, Director of Personnel Services, San Francisco Unified School District, San Francisco, Calif. (Mar. 20, 1972).

The earliest published recital of Anderson's career that I have been able to locate — " 'What Price Glory' and Its Authors," *New York Times*, Sept. 14, 1924, VIII, 2 (unsigned but based on an interview with Anderson or Stallings or both) — reads that after the Whittier professorship "teaching became irksome" and Anderson found newspaper work in San Francisco. Polytechnic is not mentioned at all. I have checked in vain for Anderson letters bearing on that school.

44. Unsigned sketches of new teachers in *Whittier College Bulletin*, XII (Aug., 1917), 8.

45. Full title: *A Stanford Book of Verse 1912–1916*. The English Club of Stanford University, 1916. Some thirty-six poems, in addition to those in the Stanford anthology, were printed in *You Who Have Dreams*. Journals in which his poems saw print over the years include *The Chapbook, The Conning Tower, The Freeman, Ladies' Home Journal, The Measure, The Nation, The New Republic, New Yorker, Scholastic, Smart Set*, and *Youth*. The 1912 issue of *The Dacotah* (University of North Dakota student yearbook) contained two of his poems. See Note 24, preceding.

46. See his pessimistic essay "Incommunicable Literature" in *The Dial*, LXV (Nov. 2, 1918), 370.

47. My information on the social and political climate at Whittier College comes from a series of letters to me from Dr. Paul S. Smith, Sept. 30, 1971 (who, as later president of Whittier, had arrived there soon after the Anderson episode); and From Dr. Charles W. Cooper, Oct. 4, 1971, and Feb. 1, 1972. I have also consulted Cooper's *Whittier*.

48. For materials relating to Anderson's teaching and his support of Camp, I am indebted to Cooper's *Whittier*, pp. 127–32, and to his research notes for that book which he has generously supplied me.

49. Cooper's taped interviews with M. Kimber and R. C. Hunnicutt, who were long-time friends of his and who are now dead. The tapes have been erased. — Cooper's letter of Feb. 1, 1972, to me.

50. Cooper's *Whittier*, p. 131.

51. Deutsch, pp. 1, 5; *Quaker Campus*, Apr. 18, 1918. — Cooper's research notes, which do not supply author and title.

52. *Whittier News*, Whittier, Calif., May 10, 1918. — Cooper's research notes, which do not supply author and title.

53. Cooper's *Whittier*, p. 132.

54. I am indebted to Dr. Cooper for first pointing out via his notes these references to Quakers.

55. Deutsch, pp. 1, 5; Sedgwick, p. 55.

56. Sedgwick, p. 54.

57. "By Way of Preface: The Theatre as Religion," *New York Times*, Oct. 26, 1941, Drama Section, p. 1.

58. "A Character Study of the Most Talked of Playwright in America . . . ," p. 25. Also, *Current Biography* (1942), pp. 20–21.

59. Alan Anderson letters to me of Jan. 15, 1972, and Apr. 16, 1973.

60. Foreword, *The Star-Wagon* in *The Best Plays of 1937–38*, ed. Burns Mantle (New York, 1938).

61. Raymond T. B. Hand, "Maxwell Anderson's House," *House Beautiful*, LXXVIII (Aug., 1936), 36–37. But Elmer Rice, who knew Anderson, calls this a "costly, ugly house," in *Minority Report: An Autobiography* (New York, 1963), p. 391.

62. By carbon monoxide poisoning in her car parked in the closed garage at home, about Mar. 22. 1953. Details of the breakup and motivation for suicide come from Alan Anderson letters to me of Jan. 15, 1972, and Apr. 16, 1973. However, Maurice Zolotow in his *Stagestruck: The Romance of Lynn Fontanne and Alfred Lunt* (New York, 1965), p. 179, quotes Lynn Fontanne as presenting a conflicting version: Mab killed herself because of jealousy of Maxwell's supposed affair with "a sixteen or seventeen year old girl." Mab's affair is not mentioned. I have checked personally with Fontanne, John F. Wharton, and Lela Chambers on this version but find no evidence to support it. Miss Fontanne, who admits to disliking Anderson, refuses to furnish me with proof for her charge, or even to discuss it. More than likely, *after* Mab proved unfaithful, Anderson sought consolation in California in the company of another woman, for instance Gilda Oakleaf, who was at that time exceptionally youthful-looking yet far from being a teenager; and this new relationship might have aggravated Mab's feeling of rejection. John F. Wharton in his letter to me of Aug. 22, 1975, says he is certain that after Mab's infidelity, Anderson looked elsewhere for solace — but did not chase young girls. (Wharton was Anderson's business associate at the time.)

63. Unsigned, "Playwright Buys Home," *New York Times*, July 24, 1955, VIII, 2.

64. Alan Anderson letter to me of Oct. 27, 1970.

65. Robert Rice, p. 24.

66. Details on Anderson's motivation for writing his first commercial play are found mainly in his *New York Times* essays "A Confession" and "By Way of Preface . . . ." Also, in Alan Anderson's letter to me of Oct. 27, 1970. Slight discrepancies occur in these accounts.

67. "A Prelude to Poetry in the Theatre," *The Essence of Tragedy and Other Footnotes and Papers* (Washington, D.C., 1939), p. 37. Essay first published as a preface to *Winterset* in 1935.

68. Contrary to what John L. Toohey writes in *A History of the Pulitzer Prize Plays* (New York, 1967), p. 109, "White Desert" was not, or certainly did not remain, Anderson's favorite play — far from it. Anderson himself wrote in "By Way of Preface . . . ," p. 1, that the play deserved to fail on the stage. This was not just false modesty. One of the last things he wrote was that he omitted to print "White Desert" in his latest collection for the reason that the play amounted to nothing as drama or in significance. — "Preface," *Four Verse Plays* (New York, 1959), p. v.
In the text of this book all dates for his plays refer to the first stage presentation unless otherwise indicated. New York productions are covered in W. P. Covington III's "A Maxwell Anderson Bibliography with Annotations," unpublished masters thesis, University of North Carolina, 1950, pp. 146–204.

69. From *Catalogue:* "the question mark which is usually placed at the end of the title does not appear in the drafts [of the play] or in the first edition . . ."(11). Accordingly, I do not use the question mark.

70. Robert Rice, p. 24.

71. Robert E. Sherwood, " 'White Desert' to 'Bad Seed,' " *Theatre Arts*, XXXIX (Mar., 1955), 28. The incident is told also in John Mason Brown, *The Worlds of Robert E. Sherwood Mirror to His Times 1896–1939* (New York, 1965), p. 163.

72. Although the stage version of "Gypsy" used the suicide ending, Anderson's original script had Ellen cut off the gas and respond gratefully to Wells' call. — Burns Mantle, ed. *The Best Plays of 1928–29* (New York, 1929), p. 315.

73. Mab acted also the role of Judith in *High Tor*.

74. "Sic Semper," *The New Republic*, XII (Sept. 8, 1917), 169.

75. *Second Overture* in *Stage*, XV (Mar., 1938), 41–45; reprinted in *Eleven Verse Plays* 1929–1939 (New York, 1940).

76. Avery, *Catalogue*, p. 36.

77. Aired on an all-network program on a Saturday evening in March, 1942. — *Current Biography* (1942).

78. Robert Rice, p. 25. Also, Maxwell Anderson letter of Feb. 28, 1942, to Viola Paradise.

79. Allan G. Halline, "Maxwell Anderson's Dramatic Theory," *American Literature*, XVI (May, 1944), 63–81; Mabel Driscoll Bailey, *Maxwell Anderson The Playwright as Prophet* (New York, 1957); and Arthur M. Sampley, "Theory and Practice in Maxwell Anderson's Poetic Tragedies," *College English*, V (May, 1944), 412–18.

80. Avery, *Catalogue*, pp. 21–22. Halline, pp. 64, 73–74, gives a convincing argument that *Mary of Scotland* marks the turning point.

81. "Poetry in the Theatre," p. 50.

82. "Off Broadway," *Off Broadway*, p. 28.

83. "Whatever Hope We Have," *The Essence of Tragedy*, pp. 21–22.

84. Allan G. Halline, p. 69.

85. "Yes, By the Eternal," *The Essence of Tragedy*, pp. 49–50.

86. John Gassner, *The Theatre in Our Times* (New York, 1954), p. 59.

87. "The Essence of Tragedy," *The Essence of Tragedy*, pp. 6–8.

88. "Off Broadway," *Off Broadway*, pp. 24–25.

89. "The Uses of Poetry," *Off Broadway*, p. 90.

90. "Whatever Hope We Have," p. 36.

91. Gerald Rabkin, *Drama and Commitment Politics in the American Theatre of the Thirties* (Bloomington, Ind., 1964), p. 274.

92. Anderson letter of Sept. 2, 1937, to Hazel A. Reynolds. — *Catalogue*, p. 125.

93. From "A Foreword by the Playwright" in a pamphlet entitled *Maxwell Anderson Festival* issued by the University of North Dakota in announcing the presentation of *Mary of Scotland* and *Elizabeth the Queen* there in late 1958. The Foreword is dated Sept. 29, 1958.

94. Sedgwick, p. 56.

95. In Anderson's letter of Mar. 15, 1948, to Alan Paton he confesses that *Cry, the Beloved Country* was the first novel he had read in many years. Alan Anderson writes: "And of course he read a great deal — biography and history — not novels." — letter to me (Oct. 27, 1970). But Anderson liked Charles Dickens greatly.

96. Robert Rice, p. 25.

97. Alan Anderson letter of Oct. 27, 1970, to me; Maurice Zolotow, *Stagestruck*, p. 179; Theresa Helburn, *A Wayward Quest* (Boston, 1960), pp. 240–41.

98. "Poetry in the Theatre," *Off Broadway*, p. 50.

99. "A Prelude to Poetry in the Theatre," *The Essence of Tragedy*, p. 33.

100. Avery, "The Maxwell Anderson Papers," p. 26.

101. "Poetry in the Theatre," *Off Broadway*, p. 50.

102. "Kurt Weill," *Theatre Arts*, XXXIV (Dec., 1950), 58.

103. Maxwell Anderson letter to Mrs. Keehn, dated Apr. 21, 1934.

104. John Gassner, "Anchors Aweigh: Maxwell Anderson and Tennessee Williams," *Theatre Time*, I (Spring, 1949), 8.

105. The Muni and Robeson letters are dated Dec. 31, 1938, and Mar. 3, 1939, respectively.

106. "Playwright Tells Why He Wrote 'Joan' and How He Signed His Star," *New York Times*, Dec. 1, 1946, II, 3. Anderson letters to Bergman, Apr. 23 and Oct. 20, 1945, respectively.

107. The diary entries on Harrison, Meredith, and Hayes are summarized in *Catalogue*, pp. 138–39. The following attest to Anderson's having conceived *High Tor* and *The Star-Wagon* for Burgess to act in: Unsigned, "Mounting 'High Tor,'" *New York Times*, Feb. 14, 1937, X, 2; Burns Mantle, ed., *The Best Plays of 1937–38* (New York, 1938), p. 6.

108. Sedgwick says *never* (p. 56). But his practice might have changed since 1936.

109. Sedgwick, who might have viewed some of the ledger-bound scripts, misunderstood the practice, for she reported that he never re-wrote a draft (56). The drafts that I saw at the University of Texas clearly show changes in some instances.

110. Accounts are found in Elmer Rice's *Minority Report*, pp. 375–77; in Sherwood's " 'White Desert' to 'Bad Seed,'" pp. 28–29, 93; and especially in John F. Wharton's *Life among the Playwrights* (New York, 1974). Wharton was for many years legal counsel for The Playwrights' Producing Company.

111. Anderson's letter of Sept. 2, 1937, to Hazel A. Reynolds.

112. Unsigned, "Anderson Has Avoided the Spotlight," *Brooklyn Eagle*, Jan. 12, 1936; Robert Rice; Sedgwick; Alan Anderson (letters to me, Oct. 27, 1970, and Apr. 16, 1973, and telephone interview with me, Apr. 8, 1973); and Prof. Lee Norvelle, of Indiana University (letter to me, Aug. 29, 1970). Norvelle, who was chairman of the National Theatre Conference New Play Project, had frequent communications with Anderson following their first meeting late in 1941. He writes: "I never knew a more humble man nor one with greater integrity. In all of my dealings with him he was kind, considerate, cooperative and trustworthy." John F. Wharton writes that, though Anderson looked like a "loveable tame bear [,] . . . he could be as violent as the wildest of wild bears." Moreover, "He was mercurial, at times a bit paranoid . . ." (6).

113. Anderson letter to the critic John Mason Brown *circa* 1937. — *Catalogue*, p. 108.

114. Two Anderson letters to Norvelle, *circa* 1942 and June 16, 1942, respectively. — *Catalogue*, p. 122.

115. "More Thoughts about Dramatic Critics," *New York Herald Tribune*, Oct. 10, 1948.

116. "Stage Money," *Colliers*, LXXIX (May 28, 1927), 24; and "More Thoughts about Dramatic Critics."

117. Elmer Rice, *Minority Report*, pp. 376, 380.

118. "More Thoughts about Dramatic Critics."

119. Howard Taubman, *The Making of the American Theatre* (New York, 1965), pp. 206, 283, 289.

120. Avery, "The Maxwell Anderson Papers," pp. 27–28.

121. Unsigned, "Maxwell Anderson Calls Drama Critics 'Jukes Family,' " *New York Herald Tribune*, Mar. 4, 1946.

122. "More Thoughts about Dramatic Critics." A good survey of his main points is found in "Thoughts about the Critics," *Off Broadway*, pp. 3–11.

123. Avery, "The Maxwell Anderson Papers," p. 27.

124. Maxwell Anderson, " 'Cut is the Branch that Might Have Grown Full Straight,' " *Off Broadway*, p. 72.

125. John Mason Brown, "What a Playwright Must Be in Order to Survive," *New York Post*, Apr. 3, 1937, quoting from Anderson's acceptance speech when he won the Drama Critics Circle Award for *High Tor*.

126. Alan Anderson letter of Oct. 27, 1970, to me. The firm Anderson House did not earn any profits. — Alan Anderson letter of Jan. 15, 1972, to me.

127. Wharton, p. 124.

128. Clyde Harold Bassett, "The Playwrights' Producing Company, Inc., 1938–1960," unpublished doctoral dissertation, University of Wisconsin, 1965, p. 501. Bassett's economic study is based on first-hand research among The Playwrights' Producing Company papers that are now filed at the Wisconsin Center for Theatre Research (The State Historical Society of Wisconsin), Madison, Wisconsin. Even more illuminating about Anderson's role in the Company is Albert Claude Gordon's "A Critical Study of the History and Development of The Playwrights' Producing Company," unpublished doctoral dissertation, Tulane University, 1965; and especially Kay I. Johnson's "Playwrights as Patriots: A History of the Playwrights' Producing Company, 1938–1960," unpublished doctoral dissertation, University of Wisconsin, 1974; both of these studies draw upon the forementioned archives.

129. Quentin Anderson letter to me of May 17, 1971; also, Wharton, p. 273.

130. "A Confession," p. 7; S. N. Behrman, "Playwrights' Company," *People in a Diary: A Memoir* (Boston, 1972), p. 220.

131. S. N. Behrman, p. 221.

Chapter Two

1. Patricia Ann Bartlett in her unpublished masters thesis (University of Idaho, 1957), "The Use of History in the Plays of Maxwell Anderson" (p. 26), is wrong in assuming that Martha spent January at Valley Forge and, therefore, that the Mrs. Morris incident is "highly improbable." Samuel

Blaine Shirk makes the same slip in *The Characterizations of George Washington in American Drama since 1875* (Philadelphia, Pa., 1949), p. 39. Actually, Martha first arrived in early February, for which see James Thomas Flexner, *George Washington in the American Revolution c.1775–1783* (Boston, 1968), p. 282; also, Douglas Southall Freeman's *Washington* abridged by Richard Harwell from the 7-vol. *George Washington* (New York, 1968), p. 375.

2. Flexner, p. 281. Opposing evidence is offered in Washington's letters to Capt. Henry Lee (Feb. 25), to James Mease (Feb. 27), and to The Committee of Congress (Feb. 29 [28]) reproduced in *The Writings of George Washington from the Original Manuscript Sources 1745–1799*, ed. John C. Fitzpatrick, Vol. X (Washington, D. C., 1933), 513, 523, 530.

3. *Valley Forge* (Washington, D. C., 1934).

4. On file at the University of Texas, Anderson letter of Mar. 20, 1934, to William A. Slade, Director of the Folger Shakespeare Library, shows that Slade had forwarded to Anderson some books dealing with George Washington and the American Revolution during the time *Valley Forge* was written. — *Catalogue*, p. 127.

5. Mabel D. Bailey, p. 63.

6. John H. Lawson, *Theory and Technique of Playwriting and Screenwriting* (New York, 1949), p. 151.

7. Gerald Rabkin, p. 284.

8. Unsigned, *Newsweek*, IV (Dec. 22, 1934), 24.

9. William E. Taylor, "Maxwell Anderson: Traditionalist in a Theatre of Change," *Modern American Drama: Essays in Criticism* (Deland, Fla., 1968), p. 50.

10. Alan Anderson letter of Oct. 27, 1970, to me.

11. Unsigned, " 'What Price Glory' and its Authors," *New York Times*, Sept. 14, 1924, VIII, 1.

12. Unsigned, "Car Kills Case, War's Original 'Captain Flagg,' " *New York Herald Tribune*, Dec. 11, 1933. Case greatly resented being called "Captain Flagg" even in jest.

13. Avery, *Catalogue*, p. 10.

14. For example, Kenneth MacGowan, *Famous American Plays of the 1920's* (New York, 1967), p. 18.

15. The earliest printed account of the collaboration is " 'What Price Glory' and its Authors" (see note 11 above). A reprint with essentially the same information appears as "How a 'Great' Play is Written Co-authors of 'What Price Glory' Review its History," *Current Opinion*, LXXVII (Nov., 1924), 617–18. In "A Confession," written late in life, Anderson supplies some details about the collaboration, and these conflict in slight ways with the 1924 accounts. Maybe his memory was slipping.

16. Anonymous, " 'What Price Glory' and its Authors," p. 1.

17. Anonymous, "Obituary." Also, Anderson, "A Confession," p. 7.

18. Hagan, "Frederick H. Koch and North Dakota . . . ," pp. 83–84.

19. Maxwell Anderson and Laurence Stallings, *What Price Glory* in *Three American Plays* (New York, 1926).

20. Jordan Y. Miller, "Maxwell Anderson: Gifted Technician," *The Thirties: Fiction, Poetry, Drama,* ed. Warren French (Deland, Fla., 1967), p. 186.

21. Burns Mantle, ed., *The Best Plays of 1924–25* (New York, 1925), p. 30.

22. Barrett H. Clark, *An Hour of American Drama* (Philadelphia, Pa., 1930), p. 90.

23. Robert P. Wilkins, "Editor's Notes," *North Dakota Quarterly,* XXXVIII (Winter, 1970), 91; Unsigned, "U. S. Prosecutor Takes No Action against War Play," *New York World,* Sept. 27, 1924.

24. Unsigned, "Censors of 'Glory' Hit from the Pulpit," *New York World,* Oct. 27, 1924, p. 28.

25. Letter from Maxwell Anderson to Kate Klugston, of Nov. 13, 1939. — *Catalogue,* p. 109.

26. Jordan Y. Miller, p. 191.

27. *Key Largo,* p. 113 (II) in *Eleven Verse Plays, 1929–1939* (New York, 1940). Hereinafter, all page citations in connection with the published verse plays will refer to this book unless otherwise indicated.

28. *Ibid.*, p. 114 (II).

29. Avery, "The Maxwell Anderson Papers," p. 31.

30. Robert Rice, p. 24. Anderson did, however, see at least one of the later Broadway productions with his guest Lee Norvelle, who at that time was handling the amateur production rights. — Lee Norvelle letter of Jan. 18, 1973, to me.

31. *The Eve of St. Mark* (Washington, D. C., 1942).

32. Marion Hargrove, *See Here, Private Hargrove* (New York, 1942), pp. ix–xi.

33. Robert Rice, p. 25.

34. Sgt. Lloyd Shearer's article in the *New York Times,* Oct. 4, 1942, VIII, 1. Details about the Fort Bragg visit and about these soldiers stem from Shearer's article and from Anderson's Foreword to *See Here, Private Hargrove.*

35. Avery, *Catalogue,* p. 39. In "The Maxwell Anderson Papers" (23), Avery notes that letters from Mulvehill and Hargrove to Anderson show personalities identifiable with their counterparts in *The Eve of St. Mark.* Also, see Robert Rice (25). The reader can easily learn in Anderson's Foreword to *See Here, Private Hargrove* that Hargrove's device of the "holding company," whereby his friends handle all his money, suggested Marion's quite similar arrangement in the play.

36. Robert Rice, p. 25.

37. Anderson himself was said to be dissatisfied with the Pacific war

scenes, for they "seemed to him to lack authenticity." — Philip Stevenson, p. 1.
38. Lee Norvelle letter of Aug. 29, 1970, to me.
39. Mabel D. Bailey, p. 119.
40. Lewis Nichols' review in *New York Times*, Jan. 12, 1944, II, 28; Rosamond Gilder's review in *Theatre Arts*, XXVIII (Mar., 1944), 133.
41. Two letters to General Dwight D. Eisenhower, dated July 1, 1943, and a later undated one. — *Catalogue*, pp. 110–11.
42. *Storm Operation* (Washington, D. C., 1944).
43. Avery, *Catalogue*, p. 41. Avery covers the whole censorship matter in pp. 41–43.
44. Laurence G. Avery, "Maxwell Anderson: A Changing Attitude toward Love," *Modern Drama*, X (Dec., 1967), 245–46.
45. Avery, *Catalogue*, p. 136.
46. *Ibid.*, p. 98.
47. *Truckline Cafe* (New York, 1946).
48. Alan Anderson telephone interview with me on Mar. 12, 1972.

Chapter Three

1. *Barefoot in Athens* (New York, 1951), pp. vii–xvi; "Notes on Socrates," *New York Times*, Oct. 28, 1951, II, 1–3.
2. John Mason Brown, "Socrates without Plato," *Saturday Review of Literature*, XXIV (Nov. 24, 1951), 27–28.
3. "Whatever Hope We Have," p. 45.
4. Mabel D. Bailey, p. 84.
5. *Ibid.*, p. 96.
6. Avery, *Catalogue*, p. 139.
7. Karl R. Popper, *The Open Society and its Enemies*, 5th ed. (Princeton, N. J., 1966), I, 189. The quoted passage is typical of what is found in the early editions.
8. Jackson K. Hershbell, "The Socrates and Plato of Maxwell Anderson," *North Dakota Quarterly*, XXXVIII (Winter, 1970), 49–53.
9. Papers of The Playwrights' Producing Company, Wisconsin Center for Theatre Research (The State Historical Society of Wisconsin), Madison, Wisconsin. "Notes for Barefoot in Athens" is excerpted in Johnson's dissertation (see next note).
10. Kay Irene Johnson, "Playwrights as Patriots: A History of The Playwrights' Producing Company, 1938–1960," unpublished doctoral dissertation, University of Wisconsin, 1974. Pp. 477–78.
11. "That Socrates went barefooted is based on passages in the *Phaedrus* and *Symposium* of Plato . . . [but] Zenophon [in *Memorabilia*] put sandals on Socrates." — Hershbell, p. 55.
12. Arthur Maurice Woodward and William George Forrest, "Sparta,"

The Oxford Classical Dictionary, ed. N. G. L. Hammond and H. H. Scullard, 2nd ed. (Oxford, 1970), p. 1007.

13. Johnson dissertation, pp. 481–82, excerpting a Maxwell Anderson letter to Victor Samrock, Nov. 20, 1951 (Papers of The Playwrights' Producing Company, box #twenty-two).

14. *The Golden Six* (New York, 1961).

15. From my telephone interview with Alan Anderson, April 8, 1973.

16. Maxwell Anderson, "Playwright Tells Why He Wrote 'Joan' and How He Signed His Star," *New York Times*, Dec. 1, 1946, II, 3.

17. Avery, *Catalogue*, p. 44.

18. *Joan of Lorraine* (Washington, D. C., 1946).

19. Avery, *Catalogue*, p. 44.

20. Eric Bentley, *In Search of Theatre* (New York, 1953), p. 8.

21. J. W. Krutch, "Drama," *The Nation*, CLXIII (Dec. 7, 1946), 642.

22. *Anne of the Thousand Days* (New York, 1948).

23. "How a Play Gets Written: Diary Retraces the Steps," *New York Herald Tribune*, Aug. 21, 1949, V, 2.

24. *Ibid*.

25. Bartlett, p. 6. Confirmed in other sources.

26. Letter from Gertrude Anderson of May 23, 1950, to Dorothy Dohm.

27. Harold Clurman, *Lies Like Truth* (New York, 1948), p. 35.

28. Brooks Atkinson, review in *Theatre Arts*, XXXIX (Mar., 1955), 28.

29. "How a Play Gets Written . . . ," p. 2.

30. Avery, *Catalogue*, p. 131. Some other details about the suit are found in "Maxwell Anderson Files Libel Action," *Publishers Weekly* (June 4, 1949), p. 2301.

31. Helen Hayes and Lewis Funke, *A Gift of Joy* (Philadelphia, 1965), pp. 127–28.

32. The actual period was from Aug., 1561 (Leith, Scotland) to some time in 1568 (Carlisle Castle, England).

33. *Mary of Scotland* (Washington, D. C., 1933).

34. "To [Prof. O. G.] Libby — and to Anderson [at the University of North Dakota] — Mary was less of a she-devil than some historians painted her. And conversely, Elizabeth was in their eyes less of a 'virgin saint' than many historians thought — or wrote." — C. L. Robertson letter of Mar. 3, 1972, to me.

35. Edith J. R. Isaacs, "Good Playing A-Plenty," *Theatre Arts*, XVIII (Jan., 1934), 18.

36. John Gassner, *Dramatic Soundings* (New York, 1968), p. 312.

37. Sampley, "Theory and Practice in Maxwell Anderson's Poetic Tragedies," pp. 412–18.

38. Lytton Strachey, *Elizabeth and Essex: A Tragic History* (New York, 1928).

39. Maurice Zolotow, *Stagestruck*, p. 177.

40. Most of the foregoing points occur in Bartlett (12, 15–16, *et passim*). I have taken the precaution of checking also Strachey's *Elizabeth and Essex* plus other sources.

41. Still another Anderson verse play about Queen Elizabeth exists, never acted or published, under the title "The Masque of Queens." Avery summarizes the plot on pp. 73–74 of his *Catalogue*. As Anderson admits in a letter to his daughter Hesper, dated May 5, 1954, the year when the play was completed, there is not much of a love story nor much action either. The play shows the kind of empty life Elizabeth leads now that normal human relationships are denied her, and she is unable to have any effective role in controlling the events of history. Near the end she has a stroke. "The Masque of Queens," like *The Golden Six*, is a bitter commentary on the futility of rulership.

42. I disagree with Allan Halline (73) who believes that *neither* character is changed for the better.

43. Anita Block, *The Changing World in Plays and Theatre* (Boston, 1939), p. 240.

44. Anderson, "A Confession," p. 7.

45. "Preface to the Politics of *Knickerbocker Holiday*," pp. v–viii of Maxwell Anderson and Kurt Weill's *Knickerbocker Holiday: A Musical Comedy in Two Acts* (Washington, D. C., 1938).

46. Unsigned, "Dutch in the Forties," *New York Times*, Sept. 25, 1938, IX, 1–2.

47. David Ewen, *New Complete Book of the American Musical Theater* (New York, 1970), p. 280.

48. By 1954 this song made *Knickerbocker Holiday* the most profitable of all of Anderson's works. — Anderson, "A Confession," p. 7.

49. Elmer Rice, *Minority Report*, p. 380.

50. Unsigned, "Roosevelt at Operetta [*sic*], Laughs at Sallies of 'Peter Stuyvesant' Twitting Government," *New York Times*, Oct. 16, 1938, I, 3. Report dated Oct. 15 (Washington). The audience in its laughter went beyond the intent of the play by interpreting this "letter" as alluding to a certain recent communication by the chief executive — most probably his urgent (and vain) appeal of Sept. 26th to Chancellor Hitler and President Benes that they settle the German-Czech dispute by negotiation rather than war. A lucky hit by Anderson.

51. Unsigned, "Benefit Performance for German Refugees," *New York Times*, Nov. 21, 1938, I, 4.

52. Laurence G. Avery, "Maxwell Anderson and *Both Your Houses*," *North Dakota Quarterly*, XXXVIII (Winter, 1970), 20.

53. Tempe E. Allison, "The Pasadena Summer Festival," *Players Magazine*, XVI (Oct., 1939), 10. In 1939, the Pasadena Playhouse ran its Midsummer Drama Festival (June 26 to Aug. 19) devoted entirely to staging Andersonia: *Elizabeth the Queen, Valley Forge, The Wingless Victory,*

The Masque of Kings, Both Your Houses (slightly revised), *Gods of the Lightning, Winterset,* and *The Star-Wagon.*

54. Stark Young, "Fourth Theatre Guild," *The New Republic,* XC (Mar. 3, 1937), 112.

55. *The Masque of Kings* in *Eleven Verse Plays,* p. 10.

56. Jordan Y. Miller, p. 188.

57. Mitchell, p. 35.

58. Letter from Gertrude Anderson of Mar. 22, 1947, to William Sloane.

59. Barrett Clark and George Freedley, *A History of Modern Drama* (New York, 1947), p. 696.

60. Cited in Caspar Harold Nannes, *Politics in the American Drama* (Washington, D. C., 1960), p. 109.

61. Anderson letter of June 9, 1949, to his lawyer, Samuel J. Silverman. — *Catalogue,* pp. 126–27.

62. *Both Your Houses* (New York, 1933).

63. John H. Lawson, *Theory and Technique of Playwriting and Screenwriting,* p. 149.

64. The following discussion of the various versions of *Both Your Houses* is mostly a summary of the scholarship of Avery as reported in his *Catalogue* and, especially, "Maxwell Anderson and *Both Your Houses.*" He is the only scholar who has studied and written about these unpublished versions up until now. The unpublished drafts are filed at the University of Texas.

65. This 1939 version is described by Avery in "Maxwell Anderson and *Both Your Houses,*" pp. 23–24.

66. *Ibid.,* p. 16. See *Catalogue,* pp. 62–82, for descriptions of the unpublished plays at the University of Texas.

Chapter Four

1. It was reportedly staged by amateurs in 1932 at the University of Minnesota, and in 1936 at Syracuse University. Sawyer Falk, Professor of Drama at the latter institution, wrote to V. M. Gilbert on Feb. 8, 1938, that the play was " 'exceptionally well received' " there. — Vedder Morris Gilbert, "Maxwell Anderson, His Interpretation of Tragedy in Six Poetical Dramas," unpublished masters thesis, Cornell University, 1938, pp. 19–20. Probably the reason Anderson never published the work is that he intended to revise it. — Letter from Anderson's secretary, Alfred C. Sturt, to unknown person (Mar. 3, 1937). Also, Barrett H. Clark's *Maxwell Anderson, The Man and His Plays* (New York, 1933), p. 30. Copies of "Sea-Wife" are owned by New York Public Library, Stephen F. Austin State University Library, and the present writer.

2. Barrett H. Clark, *Maxwell Anderson . . . ,* p. 30.

3. Mabel D. Bailey, p. 143.

4. Joseph Wood Krutch, "More Matter and Less Art," *The Nation,* CXLIV (Jan. 9, 1937), 53–54.

5. Arthur M. Sampley, p. 414.

6. Unsigned, "Boston Protects Itself," *The Nation*, CXXVII (Dec. 5, 1928), 593.

7 Maxwell Anderson and Harold Hickerson, *Gods of the Lightning* in *Gods of the Lightning and Outside Looking In* (New York, 1928). [*Outside Looking In* is by Anderson alone.]

8. Anita Block, 239.

9. "Poetry in the Theatre," p. 54. See also his Preface to *Winterset*.

10. Anderson received the silver plaque representing the Drama Critics Circle Award on Apr. 5, 1935. At the presentation, Brooks Atkinson read a letter from Eugene O'Neill praising the group for picking Anderson's " 'splendid contribution . . . to what is finest in the American theatre.' " — O'Neill's letter appears in *New York Times*, Apr. 5, 1935; cited in Mitchell, p. 34.

11. Helen Deutsch, "When Drama and Poetry Wed, Was it To Last Forever After?" *New York Herald Tribune*, May 31, 1936, p. 1. Mitchell, on pp. 32–33, proposes convincingly that Brooks Atkinson in a drama review might have indirectly put the bug in Anderson's ear (see Atkinson review of *Mary of Scotland* in *New York Times*, Dec. 3, 1933, IX, 1).

12. Avery, *Catalogue*, p. 24.

13. *Winterset* (Washington, D. C., 1935), p. 129.

14. *Ibid.*, p. 127 (Act III). For an apt study of the meaning in this passage, see Bailey, pp. 138–39.

15. Deutsch, "When Drama and Poetry Wed . . . ," p. 2.

16. Anita Block, *The Changing World . . .* , p. 241; Mabel D. Bailey, p. 142.

17. "An American Drama," *Literary History of the United States*, ed. Robert E. Spiller, *et al.*, 3rd ed. rev. (New York, 1963), p. 1322.

18. I take exception to what Samuel Kliger urges in his "Hebraic Lore in Maxwell Anderson's *Winterset*," *American Literature*, XVIII (Nov., 1946), 219–32, about Esdras' significance. On p. 226, for example, Kliger quotes Esdras as telling Gaunt "I can put you in your way," which Kliger interprets figuratively as meaning that the rabbi can (and presumably will) show the ex-judge the way to wisdom. Actually, in the context referred to, Esdras is merely offering to show him *the way out of the neighborhood* and toward home (in the literal sense) although, granted, he might be smugly intending a figurative sense. Kliger's interpretation is doubtful because nowhere, then or later, does Esdras try to enlighten Gaunt in any philosophical or religious manner. In sum, Kliger makes Esdras seem much wiser than Anderson had intended.

19. Letter from Gertrude Anderson of Nov. 25, 1938, to Martin Maloney.

20. Kliger, "Hebraic Lore . . . ." Note: "Esdras' words have no effect on Mio except to ignite his flame of justice." Howard D. Pearce, "Job in Anderson's *Winterset*," *Modern Drama*, VI (May, 1963), 35.

21. "Whatever Hope We Have," *Off Broadway*, p. 43. This was given as an address in 1937.

22. Edward A. Wright, *A Primer for Playgoers* (Englewood Cliffs, N.J., 1958), p. 68.

23. Francis E. Abernethy, "Winterset: A Modern Revenge Tragedy," *Modern Drama*, VII (Sept., 1964), 185.

24. Danton Walker, *Spooks Deluxe Some Excursions into the Supernatural* (New York, 1956), p. 165.

25. Unsigned, "Mounting 'High Tor,'" *New York Times*, Feb. 14, 1937, X, 2.

26. Both Anderson's and Meredith's climbs are found in "Mounting 'High Tor'" (see note 25 preceding). Other *Times* articles about Van Orden and sometimes his mountain are "Neighbors Honor Owner of High Tor," June 16, 1939, I, 25; "The Savior of High Tor," June 17, 1939, I, 14; Charles Grutzner, "Look-Out Park on High Tor," Aug. 5, 1956, II, 25. *New York Herald Tribune* articles include "Elmer Van Orden, 79, is Dead; High Tor Owner Inspired Play," Feb. 20, 1942; "Hudson Society Buys High Tor for Park Use," Feb. 17, 1943; Francis Sugrue, "High Tor Sold with its Ghosts and Old House," Feb. 10, 1950 [refers to sale of Van Orden's house and of the land surrounding but not including the summit]. From the Nyack, N. Y., *Journal News*: "High Tor Land is Bought by River Group," Feb. 17, 1943; and "Palisades Park System Takes Title to High Tor . . . ," Apr. 14, 1943. Also see booklet titled "Palisades Interstate Park 1900–1960" [n. d.] issued by Palisades Interstate Park Commission, Bear Mountain, N. Y..

27. Unsigned, "High Tor Land is Bought by River Group," Nyack, N. Y., *Journal News*, Feb. 17, 1943.

28. *High Tor* in *Eleven Verse Plays*, p. 109 [Act II, Scene ii]. Play first published by Anderson House in 1937.

29. The anonymous writer of "Mounting 'High Tor,'" who seems to have gotten reliable information directly from Maxwell Anderson, gives no exact date for the hike; but he says that *High Tor* was conceived six months after the completion of *Wingless Victory*, which the *Catalogue*, drawing from the mss., dates as Oct. 11, 1935; and that he started writing the play on June 1, whereas the *Catalogue* reads May 31. All quotations and other information about the inception of the play are taken from "Mounting 'High Tor.'"

30. Danton Walker, p. 166. Just as Van Dorn had the ghost of a young woman in his life, so apparently did Van Orden. Walker in his book tells an intriguing anecdote about this latter case. Hume Dixon's eighteenth-century farmhouse, located on South Mountain Road which borders High Tor, was supposedly haunted for years by the friendly ghost of a lovely young woman dressed in linsey-woolsey; Van Orden at last identified her as that of his one-time fiancée. Van Orden's hired man Gus confirmed the identification, adding that the young woman had lived in the Hume house long ago and was "the only woman Elmer had ever loved." Gus could not

recall her name. When Walker recounted to Maxwell Anderson these details the playwright responded: " 'A fascinating yarn . . . . Oddly enough, I had never heard a word of it when I decided to write that play [*High Tor*]' " (166–68).

31. Alan Anderson letters of Apr. 24, 1974, and Jan. 1, 1975, to me.

32. "Dad joined with neighbors to fight against some serious civic problems, like the New York Trap Rock Company, which threatened to make gravel for roads out of the mountain [Little Tor] that was towered over by High Tor." Letter of Jan. 15, 1972, from Alan Anderson to me. Maxwell Anderson was honorary chairman of the local Committee to Save High Tor.

33. Jordan Y. Miller, p. 190.

34. Barrett Clark and George Freedley, *A History of Modern Drama* (New York, 1947), p. 697.

35. Alan Anderson's letter of Oct. 27, 1970, to me.

36. John Gassner, *Dramatic Soundings* (New York, 1968), p. 309.

37. George R. Kenodle, "Playwrights and Ancestors," *College English*, II (Jan., 1941), 332.

38. Alan Anderson's letter of Jan. 15, 1972, to me.

39. "A Confession," p. 7.

40. *The Star-Wagon* (Washington, D. C., 1937).

41. Alan Anderson's letters to me, Nov. 23, 1970, and Jan. 15, 1972 (this last one provided the bracketed information). In this second letter, he adds that Stephen is a composite. Carroll French died in Nov., 1971, by drowning himself.

42. Lela Chambers' Biographical Notes.

43. William March [William Edward March Campbell], *The Bad Seed* (New York, 1954), p. 220. In the corresponding scene in this novel, Rhoda calmly sits outside the *basement* door, while Leroy is inside trying to break out, and delicately licks her "ice cream stick." March's method is effectively shocking — he shows us a fully heartless Rhoda — but he makes the girl seem less clever by exposing her to public view while she ignores the calls for help nearby.

44. Maxwell Anderson, *Bad Seed* (New York, 1955).

45. Reginald Denham, "Fruit of a Bad Seed," *Theatre Arts*, XXXIX (Dec., 1955), 33.

46. Denham's figure of "two months" for the period of composition tallies roughly with the other evidence: Anderson had remarried on June 16, 1954, and Act II was completed on Aug. 9th (*Catalogue*, p. 51).

47. Denham, p. 33.

48. Mabel D. Bailey, p. 182.

49. Harold Clurman, review of *Bad Seed* in *The Nation*, CLXXIX (Dec. 25, 1954), 556.

50. Elmer Rice, *Minority Report: An Autobiography* (New York, 1963), p. 394.

Chapter Five

1. "A Prelude to Poetry in the Theatre," preface to *Winterset* (Washington, D. C., 1935), p. xi.
2. Laurence G. Avery, "Maxwell Anderson: A Changing Attitude toward Love," *Modern Drama*, X (Dec., 1967), 241–48.
3. Robert Rice, p. 26.
4. Unsigned news service article in the *Houston Chronicle* (Houston, Texas): "Nixon Contends the President is 'Sovereign' in Security Matters," Mar. 12, 1976, p. 1.
5. Anderson letter of Sept. 8, 1940, to Dorothy Thompson. — *Catalogue*, p. 128. Anderson was similarly unenthusiastic, as were the other colleagues, when Elmer Rice proposed in 1938 that The Playwrights' Producing Company form a repertory company that would train actors and in other ways raise the level of American theater. — from Albert C. Gordon's dissertation, pp. 73–76, citing Rice's memorandum in Box 7 of the Company's papers at the Wisconsin Center for Theatre Research, Madison, Wisconsin.
6. Anderson letter of Nov. 12, 1938, to Mrs. Florence B. Hult. — *Catalogue*, p. 115. Add the following to the signs of disillusionment: In a letter to John Mason Brown (Nov. 17, 1937), he complained that it had become more obvious to him each year that Broadway did not care for fine or spiritual distinctions; and that, after much study, he had concluded that he and Broadway audiences shared in common only a thin margin of overlapping taste and sympathy. — *Catalogue*, pp. 107–08. Quite likely he was at the time disgusted that audiences flocked that season to see his play *The Star-Wagon*, which he considered a "potboiler," whereas relatively few had bothered to attend his serious and dignified *The Masque of Kings* staged earlier that year.
7. Anderson, "Compromise and Keeping the Faith," *Off Broadway*, p. 76.
8. Albert C. Gordon dissertation, p. 65, citing John D. Beaufort, "Theatre Hatches New Overlords," *Christian Science Monitor Magazine* (Dec. 7, 1938), p. 5.
9. Brooks Atkinson review of *Mary of Scotland* in *New York Times*, Dec. 3, 1933.
10. John Anderson, *The American Theatre* (New York, 1938), p. 95.

Selected Bibliography

1. Poems

A Stanford Book of Verse 1912–1916. The English Club of Stanford University, 1916. Some of the poems are Anderson's.

You Who Have Dreams. New York: Simon & Schuster, 1925. (See note 45 of Ch. 1 for titles of journals in which his poetry was published.)

Notes on a Dream. Edited and with introduction by Laurence G. Avery. Austin, Texas: University of Texas, 1971.

2. Published Plays (Collections)

Three American Plays [in collaboration with Laurence Stallings]. New York: Harcourt, Brace, 1926. Contains *What Price Glory*, *First Flight*, and *The Buccaneer*.

Gods of the Lightning and Outside Looking In. New York: Longmans, Green, 1928 [*Gods* written in collaboration with Harold Hickerson].

Eleven Verse Plays, 1929–1939. New York: Harcourt, Brace, 1940. Contains *Elizabeth the Queen*, *Night over Taos*, *Mary of Scotland*, *Valley Forge*, *Winterset*, *The Wingless Victory*, *High Tor*, *The Masque of Kings*, *The Feast of Ortolans*, *Second Overture*, and *Key Largo*.

Four Verse Plays. New York: Harcourt, Brace, 1959. Contains *Elizabeth the Queen*, *Mary of Scotland*, *High Tor*, and *Winterset*.

3. Single Published Plays (Chronologically listed)

Saturday's Children. New York: Longmans, Green, 1927; acting ed., 1937.

Elizabeth the Queen. New York: Longmans, Green, 1930; New York: Samuel French, 1934, acting ed.

Night over Taos. New York: Samuel French, 1932.

Mary of Scotland. Washington, D.C.: Anderson House, 1933; New York: Samuel French, 1937, acting ed.

Both Your Houses. New York: Samuel French, 1933; acting ed., 1937. A slightly revised 1939 edition exists in ms.

Valley Forge. Washington, D.C.: Anderson House, 1934; New York: Samuel French, 1937, acting ed.

Winterset. Washington, D.C.: Anderson House, 1935; New York: Dramatists Play Service, 1937, 1946, acting ed.

Masque of Kings, The. Washington, D.C.: Anderson House, 1936; New York: Dramatists Play Service, 1938, acting ed.

Wingless Victory, The. Washington, D.C.: Anderson House, 1936; New York: Dramatists Play Service, 1936, acting ed.

Star-Wagon, The. Washington, D.C.: Anderson House, 1937; New York: Dramatists Play Service, 1948, acting ed.

High Tor. Washington, D.C.: Anderson House, 1937; New York: Dramatists Play Service, 1948, acting ed.

"Feast of Ortolans, The," *The Stage Magazine*, XV (Jan., 1938), 71–78; New York: Dramatists Play Service, 1938.

"Second Overture," *The Stage Magazine*, XV (Mar., 1938), 41–45; New York: Dramatists Play Service, 1940.

Knickerbocker Holiday: A Musical Comedy in Two Acts. Washington, D.C.: Anderson House, 1938; New York: Dramatists Play Service, 1938, 1944, acting ed. [in collaboration with Kurt Weill].

Key Largo. Washington, D.C.: Anderson House, 1939.

Journey to Jerusalem. Washington, D.C.: Anderson House, 1940.

Miracle of the Danube, The, in *The Free Company Presents.* Comp. by James Boyd. New York: Dodd, Mead, 1941.

Candle in the Wind. Washington, D.C.: Anderson House, 1941.

Eve of St. Mark, The. Washington, D.C.: Anderson House, 1942.

Your Navy, in *This is War!* New York: Dodd, Mead, 1942.

Storm Operation. Washington, D.C.: Anderson House, 1944.

Letter to Jackie, in *Best Short Plays, 1943–1944.* Ed. by M. G. Mayorga. New York: Dodd, Mead, 1945.

Truckline Cafe. New York: Dodd, Mead, 1946. Martha Cox in her *Maxwell Anderson Bibliography* notes that his play was probably published (it was listed in *Cumulative Book Index*) but then withdrawn. Neither she nor I have been able to find a copy other than the typescript in the Library & Museum of the Performing Arts, New York Public Library.

Joan of Lorraine. Washington, D.C.: Anderson House, 1946; New York: Dramatists Play Service, 1947, rev. acting ed.

Joan of Arc. [Screen version of *Joan of Lorraine*, in collaboration with Andrew Slot] New York: William Sloane, 1948.

Anne of the Thousand Days. New York: William Sloane, 1948; New York: Dramatists Play Service, 1950, rev. acting ed.

Lost in the Stars. New York: William Sloane, 1949 [in collaboration with Kurt Weill].

Barefoot in Athens. New York: William Sloane, 1951; Dramatists Play Service, 1952 acting ed.

Bad Seed. New York: Dodd, Mead, 1955; Dramatists Play Service, 1957, rev. acting ed.

Masque of Pedagogues, The, in *North Dakota Quarterly*, XXV (Spring, 1957), 33–48.

The Golden Six. New York: Dramatists Play Service, 1961.

4. Unpublished But Complete Plays (Date in parentheses refers to year written)

"Meeting in Africa." (?) ms. University of Texas.
"Benvenuto." (1922) ms. University of Texas.
"White Desert." (1923) ms. University of Texas.
"Sea-Wife." (1924) ms. University of Texas; typescript at Library & Museum of the Performing Arts, at New York Public Library.
"Hell on Wheels." (c. 1926) ms. University of Texas.
"Chicot the King." (1926) ms. University of Texas and Library of Congress.
"Gypsy." (1927) ms. University of Texas; Library & Museum of the Performing Arts, at New York Public Library; condensed version published in *The Best Plays of 1928–29*.
"Princess Renegade, The." (1932) ms. University of Texas.
"Bastion Saint-Gervais, The." (1938) ms. University of Texas. Radio play. [related to *Key Largo*].
"Ulysses Africanus." (1939–1945) ms. University of Texas.
"Greeks Remember Marathon, The." (1944) radio play.
"Adam, Lilith and Eve." (1950) ms. University of Texas.
"Raft on the River" (also titled "River Chanty"). (1950) ms. University of Texas.
"Cavalier King." (1952) ms. University of Texas.
"Masque of Queens, The." (1954) ms. University of Texas.
"Christmas Carol, The." (1954) ms. University of Texas. Television play.
"Richard and Anne." (1955) ms. University of Texas.
"Madonna and Child." (1956) ms. University of Texas.
"Day the Money Stopped, The." (1957) ms. University of Texas.

5. Books of Criticism
The Essence of Tragedy and Other Footnotes and Papers. Washington, D.C.: Anderson House, 1939.
Off Broadway Essays about the Theatre New York: William Sloane, 1947.

6. Published Short Story
"Battle of Gibraltar, The." *Collier's*, LXXXV (May 10, 1930), 26, 31, 36, 38.

7. Unpublished Short Story
"West Coast, Night." (1947) ms. University of Texas.

8. Individual Essays and Articles
"Incommunicable Literature," *The Dial*, LXV (Nov. 2, 1918), 370.
"Stage Money," *Collier's*, LXXIX (May 28, 1927), 24, 30.
"The Arts as Motive Power," *New York Times*, Oct. 17, 1937.
"Preface." *November Hereabout*, by Amy Murray. New York: Henry Holt, 1940. Pp. xiii–xv.

"By Way of Preface: The Theatre as Religion," *New York Times*, Oct. 26, 1941, Drama Section, p. 1.

"The Basis of Artistic Creation in Literature." *The Bases of Artistic Creation*. New Brunswick, N.J.: Rutgers University Press, 1942. Various essays by Anderson, Roy Harris, Rhys Carpenter *et al*.

"From Reveille to Breakfast." (c. 1942) Unpublished radio script. Ms. University of Texas [background for *The Eve of St. Mark*].

"Foreword." *See Here, Private Hargrove*, by Marion Hargrove. New York: Henry Holt, 1942). Pp. ix–xi.

"Get Mad, America! *New York Times*, Feb. 22, 1942, I, 8.

"A Dramatist's Playbill," *New York Herald Tribune*, Sept. 19, 1943.

"Notes for a New Play," *PM's Sunday Picture News* (Jan. 9, 1944), IV, n. p. [relates to *Storm Operation*].

"How *Storm Operation* Grew," *National Theatre Conference Bulletin*, VI (Jan., 1944), 21–26.

"Playwright Tells Why He Wrote 'Joan' and How He Signed His Star," *New York Times*, Dec. 1, 1946, II, 3.

"The Mighty Critics," *New York Times*, Feb. 16, 1947, II, 1–2.

"More Thoughts about Dramatic Critics," *New York Herald Tribune*, Oct. 10, 1948, V, 1.

"Democracy's Temple," *Saturday Review of Literature*, XXXII (Aug. 6, 1949), 135.

"How a Play Gets Written: Diary Retraces Steps," *New York Herald Tribune*, Aug. 21, 1949, V, 1 [about *Anne of the Thousand Days*].

"Kurt Weill," *Theatre Arts*, XXXIV (Dec., 1950), 58.

"Notes on Socrates," *New York Times*, Oct. 28, 1951, II, 1–3.

"A Confession," *New York Times*, Dec. 5, 1954, II, 7.

"Robert E. Sherwood," *Theatre Arts*, XL (Feb., 1956), 26–27, 87.

"A Foreword by the Playwright," dated Sept. 29, 1958, in *Maxwell Anderson Festival* (pamphlet issued by Dakota Playmakers of University of North Dakota in announcing the presentation of two Anderson plays in Oct., 1958).

"Love Letter to a University," *North Dakota Quarterly*, XXXVIII (Winter, 1970), 89–90, reprinted from *University of North Dakota Alumni Review*, Dec. 5, 1958.

SECONDARY SOURCES

1. Letters and Miscellaneous

Letters from Alan H. Anderson to Alfred S. Shivers: Oct. 27, Nov. 23, 1970; Jan. 15, 1972; Jan. 26, Apr. 16 (consisting of comments written on copy of Ch. 1 of this book), May 5 (two letters), 1973; Apr. 24, 1974; Jan. 1, 1975.

Telephone interviews between Alan H. Anderson and Alfred S. Shivers: Mar. 12, 1972; Apr. 8, 1973.

Letters from Lela A. Chambers [neé Lela Blanch Anderson] to Alfred S. Shivers: Mar. 27, Apr. 8, 14, 26, May 8, 22, July 23, 1972; May 6, 29, 31, July 10, Sept. 20, 1973; Jan. 19, Aug. 13, 1975. "Lela Chambers' Biographical Notes" — 12 pp. of typed, single-spaced comments on Maxwell Anderson's ancestry and youth — arrived in the Apr. 26, 1972, letter.

2. Items About Maxwell Anderson
AVERY, LAURENCE G. *A Catalogue of the Maxwell Anderson Collection at the University of Texas*. Austin, Texas: University of Texas, 1968. Invaluable 175-page list of published and unpublished plays, letters, diaries, and other items set down according to the canons of descriptive bibliography. Well annotated. Many insights.
_____. "Maxwell Anderson: A Changing Attitude toward Love," *Modern Drama*, X (Dec., 1967), 241–48. Analyzes "Madonna and Child" for its satire on "the life based on sentimental notions about love" (248), hence, as indicating a shift in Anderson's attitude. Article difficult to evaluate because play ms. not readily accessible; but its apparent weakness lies in that such early plays as *What Price Glory*, "Gypsy," and *Saturday's Children* also approach love in an antisentimental way.
_____. "Maxwell Anderson and *Both Your Houses*," *North Dakota Quarterly*, XXXVIII (Winter, 1970), 5–24. Study of the differences between the 1933 and the 1939 versions of the play and how and why Anderson's political thinking changed. Lucid account, free of jargon; both true of other Avery articles.
BAILEY, MABEL DRISCOLL. *Maxwell Anderson The Playwright as Prophet*. New York: Abelard-Schuman, 1957. Originally a doctoral dissertation, this little book offers many brief but sensitive insights into some of the dramas. Written before some late plays had appeared. Analytical criticism only — no biography or other background material.
CARMER, CARL. "Maxwell Anderson Poet and Champion, " *Theatre Arts* XVII (June, 1933), 437–46. Early appreciation. Description of some plays. Correctly assesses importance of *Elizabeth the Queen*.
CARK, BARRETT H. *Maxwell Anderson The Man and His Plays*. New York: Samuel French, 1933. Very short pioneer study done near the opening of Anderson's golden decade. Covers only a few plays. Appreciative. Biography negligible.
COX, MARTHA. *Maxwell Anderson Bibliography*. Bibliographical Society. Charlottesville, Va.: University of Virginia, 1958. This list of 117 pages, only slightly annotated, covers fairly well many of the primary and secondary writings. Errors. No record of the unpublished plays. Pagination frequently absent. The user must supplement with the many other Anderson bibliographies found in indexes, check lists, etc.
DEUTSCH, HELEN. "A Playwright and Poet," *New York Herald Tribune*,

Sept. 22, 1935, pp. 1, 5. Like the articles by Rice and Sedgwick (see
later), this one is invaluable because based on one of the few personal
interviews. Tells about paternity, upbringing, education, firing from
Whittier, and many other bits that help round out the biographical
portrait.

GEIGER, LOUIS G., and J. R. ASHTON. "UND in the Era of Maxwell Anderson,"
The North Dakota Quarterly, XXV (Spring, 1957), 55–60. Taken from
Geiger's history of the University of North Dakota, this article is of
interest for descriptions of some presidents, teachers, cultural pro-
grams, campus customs and rules, hazing, cost of attendance.

HAGAN, JOHN P. "Frederick H. Koch and North Dakota: Theatre in the
Wilderness," *North Dakota Quarterly*, XXXVIII (Winter, 1970),
75–87. Hagan, whose doctoral dissertation was on Koch, illuminates
this germinal personality and his achievements as drama professor at
the University of North Dakota. A little about Anderson's relationship
with him. Sympathetic.

HALLINE, ALLAN G. "Maxwell Anderson's Dramatic Theory," *American
Literature*, XVI (May, 1944), 68–81. Drawing the theory from Anderson's critical essays, this work synthesizes most of the important features and tests them against what happens in the plays. Urges correctly
that *Mary of Scotland* marks the first time the Andersonian theory of
tragedy is used completely.

HEINEY, DONALD. "Maxwell Anderson," *Recent American Literature*.
Great Neck, N.Y.: Barron's Educational Series, 1958. Pp. 369–76.
Attempts to classify the plays. Some biography (mostly accurate, save
for carrying the journalistic activity up to 1928, and marrying Anderson
only twice). Good synopses of some main plays.

HERSHBELL, JACKSON K. "The Socrates and Plato of Maxwell Anderson,"
North Dakota Quarterly, XXXVIII (Winter, 1970), 45–59. From a historian's perspective, article examines carefully Anderson's attack on
Plato and Sparta as these are revealed in *Barefoot in Athens*. Points out
that Anderson did not have "any precise notion of either democracy or
communism" (49). A "must" for studying the play.

KRUTCH, JOSEPH WOOD. "An American Drama." *Literary History of the
United States*. Ed. by Robert E. Spiller *et al.*, 3rd ed., rev. New York:
Macmillan, 1963. Unfair where it describes the dramas as "theatrically
successful pastiche." Interesting comparisons with O'Neill.

MILLER, JORDAN Y. "Maxwell Anderson: Gifted Technician." *The Thirties:
Fiction, Poetry, Drama*. Ed. by Warren French. Deland, Fla.: Everett
Edwards, 1967. Miller, typical of recent critics, underrates Anderson.
He does, however, recognize the "unquestioned artistic integrity" and
rightly raises the question why Anderson is not taught more in
graduate schools.

QUINN, ARTHUR HOBSON. *A History of the American Drama from the Civil
War to the Present Day*. Rev. ed. New York: Appleton-Century-Crofts,

1936. Well-done discussion of *Mary of Scotland*. Too early to cover some of the best plays.

RICE, PATRICK J. "Maxwell Anderson and the Eternal Dream," *Catholic World*, CLXXVII (Aug., 1953), 364–70. Subtle but not always convincing arguments about Anderson's failings as a tragedian. The author (a Jesuit priest) correctly urges the need for a religious foundation in tragedy. Yet the success of much of the work remains unexplained.

RICE, ROBERT. "Maxwell Anderson: A Character Study of the Most Talked of Playwright in America Based on the First Interview He Has Granted since 1937," *PM's Sunday Picture News*, III (Nov. 29, 1942), 23–27. Perhaps the most detailed and accurate of the newspaper interviews with Anderson. Especially useful in covering the early years: the Reverend Anderson, schooling, marriage, teaching, *Bulletin*, motivation for writing first play, tastes, etc. Much of the information here is not found elsewhere.

ROBERTSON, C. L. "In the Days of Peg-Top Trousers," *The North Dakota Quarterly*, XXV (Spring, 1957), 52–54. Short, intimate, nostalgic record of what it was like to be a student, as Robertson was, at the University of North Dakota during Anderson's time. Describes the administrations of Presidents W. Merrifield and F. McVey (who is represented in Anderson's "The Masque of Pedagogues," in which Robertson acted). Author did not know Anderson well but gives a little description.

SAMPLEY, ARTHUR M. "Theory and Practice in Maxwell Anderson's Poetic Tragedies," *College English*, V (May, 1944), 412–18. Excellent in illuminating the dramatic development, in evaluating some tragedies, and in showing the insufficiency of the tragic theory alone in accounting for the success of some plays.

SEDGWICK, RUTH WOODBURY. "Maxwell Anderson, Playwright and Poet," *Stage*, XIV (Oct., 1936), 54–56. Many bits of first-hand biographical information not otherwise available in print. Perceptively written. In error about Anderson's revisions.

TAYLOR, WILLIAM E. "Maxwell Anderson: Traditionalist in a Theatre of Change." *Modern American Drama: Essays in Criticism*. Deland, Fla.: Everett / Edwards, 1968. Examines the agnosticism, pessimism, cynicism. Taylor, practically alone save for Wall and Avery, speaks of the great significance that Anderson attaches to the redeeming power of romantic love between man and woman. Mistaken about Act II of *What Price Glory* being written by Stallings.

WALL, VINCENT. "Maxwell Anderson: The Last Anarchist." *American Drama and its Critics. A Collection of Critical Essays*. Chicago: University of Chicago, 1965. In-depth study of Anderson's strange laissez faire individualism and moderate Anarchism. Many useful observations. But mistaken in saying that he seldom attended his premieres and that he owned High Tor.

WATTS, HAROLD H. "Maxwell Anderson: The Tragedy of Attrition," *College English*, IV (Jan., 1943), 220–30. Argues that Anderson uses a "tragedy of attrition," wherein the hero endures and dies, rather than the older tragedy wherein he falls and dies. Such heroes hold a noble pose in the face of an inimical world.

WHARTON, JOHN F. *Life among the Playwrights Being Mostly the Story of The Playwrights' Producing Company, Inc.* New York: Quadrangle, 1974. Scattered throughout this popularized, largely undocumented study of the Company are letters to and from the members, records of play production, insights into the usually cordial relationships among the members, and many photographs. The astute Wharton, in his roles as the Company's legal adviser and play reader, had close contacts with Anderson from 1938 onwards. Humorous, readable. Records pleasant as well as unpleasant things about Anderson's life. Valuable in any study of this playwright.

Index

171